902
JOH
W

Social psychology and modernity

Social psychology and modernity

Thomas Johansson

Open University Press
Buckingham · Philadelphia

Open University Press
Celtic Court
22 Ballmoor
Buckingham
MK18 1XW

e-mail: enquiries@openup.co.uk
world wide web: http://www.openup.co.uk

and
325 Chestnut Street
Philadelphia, PA 19106, USA

First Published 2000

A catalogue record of this book is available from the British Library

ISBN   0 335 20104 0 (pb)   0 335 20110 5 (hb)

Library of Congress Cataloging-in-Publication Data
Johansson, Thomas, 1959-
    Social psychology and modernity/Thomas Johansson.
        p. cm.
    Includes bibliographical references and index.
    ISBN 0-335-20110-5 (hb) – ISBN 0-335-20104-0 (pbk.)
    1. Social psychology. 2. Civilization, Modern – 20th century. I. Title.
HM1033.J64 2000
302–dc21

                                                                99-056500

Typeset by Type Study, Scarborough
Printed in Great Britain by Biddles Ltd, Guildford and King's Lynn

Contents

Acknowledgements

This book is the result of continuous attempts to combine two different identities. Being both a psychologist and a sociologist, I have always wished that it would be possible to avoid being either–or and instead become a both–and person. However, this is definitely a very difficult task. I have certainly not succeeded in this book. The professional person present in this text is obviously Thomas Johansson, the sociologist. But I strongly believe that Thomas Johansson, the psychologist, has contributed to the text and added some interesting flavours. So, thanks Thomas, the psychologist. I would also like to express my gratitude to Karen Williams (K.W.), who has translated the manuscript so well. Without you, the whole project would have failed altogether. Finally, I am really happy to be able to address an international audience. I hope you will enjoy this book.

Thomas Johansson

Introduction: social psychology and modernity

What is social psychology?

There are a number of definitions of what social psychology is, or ought to be. Without delving into them too deeply, we can say that the focus of most definitions is on the concept of social interaction. These definitions often include specific and interrelated questions about what is involved when people meet. In some cases, psychological factors affecting the meeting are studied; in other cases, the major focus is on the effects of the social environment. Behavioural and cognitive factors are central to the analyses made in more psychologically oriented textbooks. In an American textbook from 1985, social psychology is defined as follows:

> *Social psychology* is the scientific study of the thoughts, actions and interactions of individuals as affected by the actual, implied, or imagined presence of others. . . . Social stimuli affect the thoughts and motivations of an individual, and these internal or *intrapsychic* factors affect that individual's subsequent interactions with other people.
>
> (Tedeschi *et al*. 1985: 5, original emphasis)

Given this, we can imagine a similar, but sociologically oriented definition focused on the social environment or social institutions. Such a definition appears in a more sociologically oriented textbook from 1981: 'People are products of their environment, but they also help to shape this environment. Social psychology is a science with which the interplay between the individual and his environment is investigated'[1] (Eskola [1971] 1981: 11). Although both of these definitions of social psychology are acceptable, I would like to claim that when we use such narrow definitions, we miss something of the essence of a dynamic social psychological analysis.

The Swedish social psychologist Johan Asplund has defined social psychology as a science located on the slash between individual and society. This approach to social psychology as an intermediary area opens up a creative discussion of how social psychological studies *can* be carried out. The entire definition is as follows:

> Consider the formula 'individual/society'. What I am trying to say is that social psychology is – or should be – a science on the slash between individual and society. If this were so, it would be a science neither about the wall nor the cracks, but about the cracks in the wall.[2]
>
> (Asplund 1983: 62)

In explaining to us what social psychology is – or ought to be – Asplund uses a metaphor which points out that a complete separation of individual and societal factors is an impossibility. Therefore, we must devise concepts that allow us to move freely between different levels of abstraction and disciplines – concepts that can help us both to understand what social interaction is and, at the same time, to maintain an interest in both psychology and sociology. Thus, in order to carry out social psychological studies, we must formulate ideas that overstep the normal disciplinary boundaries and that capture something of the subtle dynamics implied in Asplund's slash.

Of interest in social psychology is an intermediary area bordering on both psychology and sociology; this area has its own character and concepts. Thus, if we use dramaturgic terminology to describe social psychology, we need a scene, actors and a good story for this type of analysis of human existence to be possible. Many of the processes we attempt to describe and analyse using social psychology are diffuse in nature. This, however, constitutes a challenge for the social psychological imagination. Herbert Blumer summarizes the problems associated with this type of analysis in the following way:

> Or, to put the matter in terms of the concepts of social psychology, we may say that such concepts are vague and ambiguous because the observations that we use to serve them are tenuous and uncertain; and that the observations have this character because of an inability to form dependable judgements and inferences; and, further, that such undependable judgements and inferences are at present intrinsic to many of the kinds of observation which we have to make and use.
>
> (Blumer 1969: 181)

The social psychological concepts we use in order to say something essential about contemporary society are often difficult to operationalize. When we try to mould these concepts into measurable phenomena, they lose part of their relevance for studies of contemporary life. Instead, the purpose of a social psychological analysis is to further the perspectivistic vision and create the conditions for a dynamic understanding of the relation between 'individual' and 'society'. Thus, those concepts that have been developed are better characterized as 'sensitizing' than as explanatory (Blumer 1954). Blumer describes the contrast between definitive and sensitizing concepts as follows:

> Whereas definitive concepts provide prescriptions of what to see, sensitizing concepts merely suggest directions along which to look. The hundreds of concepts – like culture, institutions, social structure, mores and personality – are not definitive concepts but are sensitizing in nature. They lack precise reference and have no bench marks which allow a clean-cut identification of a specific instance, and of its content. Instead, they rest on a general sense of what is relevant. There can scarcely be any dispute over this characterization.
>
> (Blumer 1954: 148)

Today's dominant view of what social psychology is differs considerably from Blumer's approach to the subject. The textbooks used in social psychology are often tied to the American, more psychologically oriented tradition. This tradition is largely based on the innumerable experiments that have been, and continue to be, carried out, in which people are subjected to various kinds of physical or psychological influences. The most famous studies in this tradition are, for example, Milgram's obedience experiments, Sherif's group experiments and Asch's conformity studies. Within this variant of social psychology, concepts such as socialization, norm, attitude, self-image, cognitive dissonance and so on are used. These notions are not employed in order to reflect upon people's everyday lives, but rather to define and operationalize various aspects of human existence.

Although my attitude towards this type of social psychology is not totally negative, I have chosen to focus on another tradition. In this tradition, a more consistent approach is used in order to frame questions about, and investigate, people's social situation and identity in relation to what is often called modernity. Before I delve into a more detailed discussion of the various traditions and authors associated with this variant of social psychology – beginning with Georg Simmel's analyses of big city life in Berlin in the year 1900 and continuing to contemporary discussions of modernity/postmodernity – I will briefly describe the growth and breakthrough of modern social psychology.

Modernity and social psychology

The end of the 1800s marked the beginning of social psychological experimentation, and early in the next century, the first two textbooks in the area were published. One was written by a sociologist and the other by a psychologist.[3] Why did this way of looking at people and society experience its breakthrough during this period in history? According to the Swedish social psychologist Johan Asplund, it was only after an industrialized and differentiated society developed that it became at all interesting to discuss and ask questions about the relation between the individual and society. It has, of course, been possible to consider this relation earlier in history. However, it was at the end of the 1800s that we were first able to discern more radical changes in this relation and a clear and more general focus on the individual's place in society, and when the development of a scientific discipline and approach – intended solely to deal with these complex relations – became relevant.

As social psychology grew and developed as a discipline, it was perhaps unavoidable that scientists began to take an interest in how individuals reacted to the social changes being studied. If we want to attribute the growth of modern social psychology to a certain point in time, we might choose the year 1892, when the world's first department of sociology was founded in Chicago. Many influential scientists worked here: for example, Albion Small, who helped to translate Georg Simmel's work; Charles Cooley, one of the founders of symbolic interactionism; and Robert Park, who built up an entire research programme in the spirit of Simmel's work; even George Herbert Mead worked at the same university. But why Chicago?

At the end of the 1800s, Chicago experienced a relatively rapid transformation into a world-class metropolis. Urbanization and immigration contributed to the shaping of an urban environment marked by pronounced differentiation of the city milieu, as well as of the people living there. We might say that most of the kinds of problems in which sociologists have taken an interest over the years – urbanization, individualization, the breakdown of the family, gang crime, youth culture, multiculturalism and so on – were concentrated in one and the same place. This combination of a creative and intellectually versatile research environment and a historical situation characterized by constant change, contributed to the creation of the conditions from which a certain type of social psychology – deeply rooted in the American culture – could develop. This mixture of philosophical speculations and ethnographic studies of strategically chosen urban cultures and social types, which characterized Chicago's intellectual environment at the time, also proved to be quite successful. It is here that we can see the roots of both symbolic interactionism and a social psychology more oriented towards cultural studies.

There would seem to be a strong connection between sweeping social change and the development of successful social psychological perspectives. While scientists in Chicago were busy with their field studies and theoretical exchanges about the interactionist point of view during the 1920s and

1930s, an intellectual environment was developing in Frankfurt, Germany. Specific to the situation in which the German researchers worked was that their society would soon begin to develop into a Fascist, totalitarian state, in which all types of intellectual and critical thinking were banned. In this environment, and in the USA, where many of these scientists sought refuge before the war broke out, a type of social psychology developed that was philosophically oriented and extremely multifaceted. If the incomprehensible events of this troubled time in history were to be understood at all – if there was to be a chance of comprehending how people could be transformed into brutal monsters – it was necessary to analyse the relation between social change and psychological factors. The social psychology that grew out of this period was marked largely by pessimism about society's subsequent development. In this book, I will return now and then to the question of social psychology's ties to psychoanalysis and different attempts to relate social change to psychoanalytic theory.

If we move on to the post-war period, we find that social psychology had become more pluralistic. Symbolic interactionism constituted an almost self-contained intellectual tradition, where a specific kind of social psychological thinking developed. At the same time, the direction that had evolved in the Frankfurt school inspired various attempts to develop this type of social psychology. We can also observe increased polarization between the more sociologically and psychologically oriented approaches to social psychology. The former variant developed more and more within the framework of sociology and in terms of problems related to actor/structure, whereas textbooks with 'social psychology' in the title tended to focus on a more psychologically oriented social psychology and certain aspects of symbolic interactionism.

As I see it, discussions of modernity have always had strong ties to social psychology. This becomes even clearer during the 1980s and 1990s, a period in which discussions of the character of modernity were revitalized. This renewal was largely dependent on the postmodern attack on the project of modernity. During this period, many books were written in which concepts such as identity, reflexivity, life project, ambivalence, risk and so on were given a partly new meaning. This revitalized theoretical interest in discussions of modernity has taken place against a backdrop of drastic changes in world politics, increased awareness about threats to the environment and human survival, and tendencies towards increased xenophobia (fear or hatred of strangers or foreigners) and neo-poverty that characterize the political climate towards the end of the twentieth century. Getting a grip on this historical transformation requires the development of a social psychological thinking that enables us to theorize about, among other things, the growth of the media, the multicultural society, postcolonialism and globalization.

In order to deepen our understanding of what is meant by contemporary social psychology, we will take a closer look at three different studies and use them as our point of departure for an analysis of the connection between social psychology and modernity.

Three social psychological studies

How is social psychology carried out?

The three cornerstones of a social psychological analysis are: individual/actor, social interaction and society/culture. In order to determine what constitutes a good social psychological study, we must consider in every case how well the author has dealt with the dynamic relation between these three factors. According to the point of view presented in this book, good social psychology is done by a researcher who is able to bring into focus what happens during a specific meeting between people. This must be accomplished without reducing the meeting to individual thoughts, feelings and experiences, or to a cultural process.

The three studies I will present in brief are all tied to historically specific analyses of modernity. The first study, *The Ghetto*, was written by Louis Wirth. It was part of an extensive mapping of the city of Chicago that was carried out within the framework of the so-called Chicago school during the 1920s and 1930s. Within this tradition, we find a number of similar studies dealing with everything from the homeless to youth gangs.[4] The second study, entitled *The Authoritarian Personality*, was the result of a far-reaching research project that was carried out by scientists tied to the Frankfurt school. This study was unique in that the researchers, in an attempt to understand the growth of Fascism and xenophobia, tried to combine psychoanalytical theory and social theory. Enormous attention was given to the study, and it brings to the fore both the advantages and disadvantages of this type of approach. Finally, we will look at Anthony Giddens' *The Transformation of Intimacy*. Giddens' point of departure is the concept of institutional reflexivity, which he uses to discuss and analyse contemporary relational patterns. Although these three studies are typical of the different time periods in which they were undertaken, there are certain similarities between them that, in my opinion, make them excellent examples of how social psychology can be carried out.

The ghetto and the stranger

Louis Wirth published his study on the ghetto in 1928. *The Ghetto* provides the reader with a history of the growth of the ghetto. In medieval Europe, Jewish neighbourhoods were called ghettos. The origin of this segregation was not the result of planning, but rather of a spontaneous search for security and cultural similarity. With time, however, the ghetto became institutionalized and, thereby, a tool that could be used by those in power to control and oppress the Jews. Wirth's interest is in how this institution has changed in different environments and at different historical points in time. His primary focus is on Chicago Jews and their adaptation to American culture at the beginning of this century.

Ghettos arise when people try to adapt themselves to what are often hostile environments. Ghettos also make it easier for the powers that be to control the strangers, while creating the conditions for solidarity between vulnerable people and for resistance against oppression. Simmel would have called the ghetto a *social form*. This social institution offered a secure environment with a solid internal hierarchy, and the regularization of social status and family life. The Jewish culture was safeguarded and formed within the ghetto's 'walls'. Wirth writes that: 'The ghetto is not only a physical fact; it is also a state of mind' (Wirth 1928: 8). It is this particular 'state of mind' that Jews carry with them on their worldwide wanderings and that results in the more or less spontaneous formation of Jewish ghettos.

Wirth provides us with a detailed description of the Jewish ghetto in Chicago. He takes us to a bygone world of shopkeepers, beggars, rabbis, conflicts between Jews and Poles, odours from the markets and a culture that would slowly but surely dissolve. We find thorough descriptions of the various social types who appeared on Maxwell Street, which was the main Jewish thoroughfare in Chicago during the 1920s. Among others, we meet the beggar (*Schnorrer*), who confirmed the religious Jews' identity by accepting gifts, and we meet *the puller*, who was an expert at stopping pedestrians and getting them to try various products in which they were actually not at all interested. Wirth describes Maxwell Street, where all these people met and were integrated, as follows:

> The noises of crowing roosters and geese, the cooing of pigeons, the barking of dogs, the twittering of canary birds, the smell of garlic and of cheeses, the aroma of onions, apples, and oranges, and the shouts and curses of sellers and buyers fill the air. Anything can be bought and sold on Maxwell Street. . . . Everything has value on Maxwell Street, but the price is not fixed. It is the fixing of the price around which turns the whole plot of the drama enacted daily at the perpetual bazaar of Maxwell Street.
>
> (Wirth 1928: 233)

Little by little, the Jews began to take an interest in the opportunities offered by American society. Wirth describes the successive dissolution of the ghetto as a physical place. Life on Maxwell Street was transformed when new groups moved in and took over these city neighbourhoods. However, although the Jews were integrated into the city, much of their distrust of non-Jews (*Goyims*) lived on, and they tried to preserve their customs and culture. After having attempted to adapt to new manners and customs, it was not uncommon for Jews to return to the synagogue and to Jewish customs. Many of the Jews who left the ghetto experienced a constant internal conflict and found it difficult to adapt to the 'world outside'. They lived in two worlds simultaneously, without feeling really at home in either of them.

The American Jews were often met with prejudices, contempt and, at times, open hostility. In order to deal with these threats, they were forced to unite. The solidarity that had developed within 'the walls' of the ghetto continued to exist outside the ghetto in the form of a mental and social state. Wirth describes how Chicago Jews collected money for various causes and how they were loyally committed to different Jewish questions. The cosmopolitan Jew always has one foot in the ghetto. He or she is drawn to what the world has to offer, but the security and culture that developed in the ghetto constitutes an important source of personal identity.

Wirth's study of the ghetto is certainly worth reading today. He succeeds in conveying images of a bygone culture, and at the same time in capturing some of the social psychological mechanisms that are engaged when people are exposed to external threats. By providing us with a historical background, careful descriptions of environments and social types, and by conveying various people's stories of how they adapted to life in, and outside, the ghetto, Wirth helps us to understand how the distinction between 'we' and 'them' develops and is maintained in different historical contexts. He offers insights into both the mechanisms of oppression and the social psychology of resistance.

The Authoritarian Personality

Studies of the authoritarian personality had begun during the 1930s. Much empirical material was collected under the direction of Erich Fromm. The idea was to study the reaction of the German working class to the growing Fascist ideology. Although never published, this study – which was based largely on a type of psychoanalytic thinking elaborated by Fromm and others – resulted in a number of books, for example, Fromm's famous study, *Escape from Freedom* (Fromm 1969). Another great theoretical and empirical project, which was a foundation for later studies of the authoritarian personality, was *Studien über Auktorität und Familie*. Among other contributions, this study consisted of a few influential theoretical essays by Horkheimer and Fromm.

While Horkheimer promoted the idea that the position of the family and the father in society had been weakened and replaced by other agents of socialization – primarily the mass media – Fromm discussed different personality types and how they might underlie a totalitarian society. He became caught up in the sadomasochistic character. This personality type included a combination of attributes such as submission to authority, tendencies towards feelings of superiority and a contempt for human weakness. According to Fromm, the only way to counteract developments towards a totalitarian society was to promote a personality development directed towards mature heterosexuality and a strong ego; thus, a personality that has successfully progressed through Freud's various stages of development, and, in other words, 'solved' its Oedipus complex. In spite of the fact that members of the Frankfurt school became more and more critical of Fromm's normative view of personality, his thoughts would shape further studies of the authoritarian personality.

The Authoritarian Personality (Adorno *et al.*) was published in 1950 in the series *Studies in Prejudice*. The purpose of this series of studies, which was financed by the Jewish Committee, was to investigate anti-Semitic and prejudicial attitudes among various social groups in post-war America. In the study just mentioned, a number of different research methods were used to analyse how people with varying social backgrounds relate to different types of minority groups. Theoretical speculations and empirical results are combined in this text of about 1000 pages. In the book's preface, Max Horkheimer writes as follows:

> This is a book about social discrimination. But its purpose is not simply to add a few more empirical findings to an already extensive body of information. The central theme of the work is a relatively new concept – the rise of an 'anthropological' species we call the authoritarian type of man. In contrast to the bigot of the older style he seems to combine the ideas and skills which are typical of a highly industrialized society with irrational and anti-rationalist beliefs. He is at the same time enlightened and superstitious, proud to be an individualist and in constant fear of not being like all the others, jealous of his independence and inclined to submit blindly to power and authority.
>
> (Adorno *et al.* 1950: ix)

The focus of this study is the *potential* Fascist individual. The basic assumption is that the individual's political, economic and social convictions form a coherent psychological pattern. This pattern, in turn, is based on a specific mentality that is a manifestation of more profound psychological character traits. From a mixture of fragments of psychoanalytic theory and speculations from culture theory, a scale was constructed for the purpose of measuring an individual's potential to become a Fascist. Now quite famous, this scale came to be called the F-scale.

The construction of the F-scale was based on earlier theoretical work and was related to the other measurement techniques used in *The Authoritarian Personality*. The scale was intended to capture a person who was rigid, masochistic, aggressive, reproachful, intense, superstitious, cynical, projecting, paranoid and so on. The personality traits corresponded well with Fromm's description of the sadomasochistic character. However, it is not readily apparent from Adorno's text how the F-scale was tied to earlier attempts to study the same type of phenomenon. Even though the three components that were used in the study – that is, the increasingly means-end, rational social order, the weakened family and the psychoanalytical discussion of the Oedipus complex – were not explicitly related to one another, the F-scale and the consideration of the authoritarian personality itself were beneficial. Rather than capturing single personality traits, the researchers succeeded in identifying a number of social psychological mechanisms that had a clear place in discussions of Fascism and contempt for minorities.

In *The Authoritarian Personality*, many people are introduced, and we are allowed to see in detail their reasoning on the issue of minorities. We are helped to understand how cognitive attitudes originate from more profound personality traits; how the fear of strangers affects the individual's ability to draw conclusions and think logically. When pressed or threatened, the potential Fascist expresses his or her xenophobic opinions much more clearly. The paranoid and psychotic complex of concepts dominating the deepest psychological levels of this person's mind are activated, the result being that, through mechanisms of projection, various social and ethnic groups are picked out as scapegoats. By not contenting himself with only the obvious content in the interview material – which, in many cases, contained great scepticism about strangers, without being openly hostile in nature – the author of this study succeeded in showing how dangerous this potential Fascism really is. One of the cognitive attitudes that Adorno dissects in his theoretical essays is the so-called 'two kinds idea'. This idea is based on people's differentiation between, for example, good Jews and bad Jews. This type of thinking is illustrated in the following excerpt from an interview with a woman:

> The Negroes are getting so arrogant now, they come to the employment office and say they don't like this kind of job and that kind of job. However, there are some who are employed at the employment office and they are very nice and intelligent. There are nice ones and bad ones among us. The Negroes who have always lived in Oakland are all right; they don't know what to do with all those who are coming in from the South either. They all carries knives; if you do something they don't like, they will get even with you, they will slice you up.
>
> (Adorno *et al.* 1950: 627)

According to Adorno, this polarized and paranoid type of thinking originates in an almost psychotic approach to reality and in a poorly solved Oedipus complex. That which is foreign or strange is experienced as unpleasant and threatening. By projecting his or her own unsolved aggression and other feelings about strangers, the individual is able to maintain a fragile inner balance. If an individual such as this is exposed to levels of external threat that are too high, there is a risk that his or her inner chaos will not only be projected on to other people, but even lead to hostile and destructive behaviour. In this way, the potential Fascist becomes active, acting out his or her inner psychotic fantasies. Adorno and his colleagues never found a solution to this problem – a problem that we still tackle today.

Self-reflexivity and open relationships

Anthony Giddens' study *The Transformation of Intimacy* is based on analyses of self-help and other relevant literature. Giddens' aim is to provide a background to, and frame questions about, contemporary Western love relationships. His point of departure is a discussion of the romantic love complex. Through this, he leads us to an examination of the growth of what he calls *pure relations*. This type of relationship must be understood against the backdrop of the radical changes that have taken place in late-modern day-to-day life and changes in how people create their own identities. Although Giddens' study is about transformations in the sphere of intimacy, even more specific questions focus on sexuality, states of dependency and, of course, the question of equality.

The main argument in Giddens' book is that the women's movement was responsible for the drastic changes observed in intimate relationships. The romantic love complex was primarily a feminine *Gestalt*. Even though this view of love relationships has mostly been understood as a part of the subordination to which women have been subjected, Giddens thinks that there is an explosiveness in this type of love that facilitates the dissolution of the super- and subordination that have long characterized the relationship between men and women. Although the consumption of love stories has been considered a manifestation of female passivity, it is possible that the fantasy worlds and desires to transform everyday life that are cultivated in these stories can contribute to changes in how intimate relationships are viewed. The individual is always central in romantic love, constantly asking herself: 'Who am I?', 'What do I want in life?', 'Who do I want to live with?', 'What is happiness?' and so on. These questions lead her straight into the type of relationship termed by Giddens as the pure relation.

Just as a given social form is transformed into another – without dissolving completely – romantic love is successively converted into the late-modern love relationship. Giddens describes this relationship as follows:

> A pure relationship has nothing to do with sexual purity, and is a limiting concept rather than only a descriptive one. It refers to a situation where a social relation is entered into for its own sake, for what can be derived by each person from a sustained association with another; and which is continued only in so far as it is thought by both parties to deliver enough satisfactions for each individual to stay within it.
>
> (Giddens 1992: 58)

The growth of the late-modern love relationship does not imply the end of love, but instead the creation of new conditions for love. It is no longer a question of finding a specific person, but developing the specific relationship.

This love relationship is based on mutual respect, open discussions about the nature of the relationship, equality and an ability to approach and discuss questions concerning feelings and relations. Achieving this requires a restructuring of the balance of power between the sexes.

However, there is another side to all this. While constituting the prerequisite for the growth of a new sphere of intimacy, this institutional reflexivity also has consequences for people's need for, and lack of, a fundamental feeling of security in their lives. Institutional reflexivity is a result of more general changes in modernity. The growth of expert systems, the increased amount of knowledge on everything from sexuality to society's energy consumption, and the acceleration of the circulation of this knowledge, results in a situation in which people develop a reflexive attitude towards their life projects and identities. The outcome of this is a constant questioning of 'truths' and a relativizing of the concept of knowledge. Thus, this development is even a threat to people's basic need for security. Reflexivity and the search for an identity can often lead to different types of dependency.

Dependency can, of course, be expressed in various ways: the alcoholic, the sexual abuser, the work addict and so on. Although manifested differently, these are all expressions of an attempt to escape the reflexive identity project. Having a dependency implies giving up the chance to choose and the ability to influence one's own life. In a society in which choosing a life plan and lifestyle is not only possible, but central, dependency constitutes a regressive behaviour that indicates a need to confine life to certain patterns; a need that can easily turn into a destructive abuse of drugs, relationships and experiences. When routines no longer give security, but instead become an unhealthy and destructive pattern of living, the individual has given up the opportunities offered by the reflexive identity project.

Giddens' aim is to analyse the possibilities as well as the limitations of the reflexive identity project, with a special focus on the transformations of intimacy. The origins of this project are in the more general changes in modernity that have been discussed by theoreticians such as Giddens, Zygmunt Bauman, Ulrich Beck and others. The individual who appears is caught between the power of traditions and habit, on the one hand, and the opportunities to elaborate various lifestyles and to choose a specific way in which to mould the life project, on the other. Thus, the individual must constantly battle with the ambivalence and irresolution that this implies.

The late-modern love relationship makes possible the growth of democratic relations, transformed gender identities and mutual respect, but also creates insecurity and leads to endeavours to re-establish traditions and stability in life. In discussing this change in the sphere of intimacy, we naturally enter into new discussions about several other societal and cultural changes and their consequences for the individual.

Gestalt and background

What unites the three studies briefly described above is their commitment to questions that concern the individual's life project and dreams. The authors attempt to frame questions about how the individual relates to changes in society. Although stressing different aspects of the interaction process, they do not reduce phenomena to pure sociology or psychology; instead, they try to create an understanding of the complex processes being studied.

It is obvious that these works are the products of different historical points in time. Wirth's study of the ghetto gives us a glimpse of a specific city environment in Chicago at the beginning of the 1900s. The strength of this study is its almost literary descriptions of people's fates and milieux, as well as its analyses of alienation and integration. What is lacking are elaborated theoretical discussions and concepts, but, in spite of this, we are provided with a good picture of the identity-creating mechanisms that were recreated in the framework of the ghetto.

In the study on the authoritarian personality, we gain some insight into the social psychological dynamics that contribute to the reproduction of a potential Fascism. The F-scale is not only a measurement tool, but also a map of the various mechanisms at work in the creation of fear of strangers and contempt for 'the other'. The strength of this study lies in its discussions of these mechanisms and in the connection between psychoanalytic theory and analyses of people's attitudes towards foreigners. The study constitutes an ambitious attempt to interrelate three different levels of analysis: the intrapsychological, the attitudinal and the societal. Although the type of Freudo-Marxism that inspired studies of the authoritarian personality has received a great deal of criticism, this way of seeing things has also affected development in social psychology and created interest in the contribution psychoanalytic theory has made to social scientific studies.

Giddens' study of the transformations of intimacy relates the contemporary discussion on reflexivity to changes in the love relationship and the increased divorce rate in the West. By experimenting with a number of concepts, for example, pure relations, reflexivity, dependency and anti-dependency, Giddens succeeds in developing a social psychological analysis of the transformations of intimacy. Many of his concepts build a bridge between the societal and psychological level. In order to understand Giddens' analysis of intimacy, we must first create for ourselves a good picture of the general societal changes that have led to increased reflexivity and to a transformation of the relations between the sexes. When we have done this, the discussion on 'pure relations' is given real meaning.

Simple recipes for how to do a social psychological analysis do not exist. The number of studies I would unconditionally describe as excellent or classic works in social psychology is rather small. In this category I would place, among others, Nels Anderson's *The Hobo* ([1923] 1967) and some of the early Chicago studies, William F. Whyte's *Street Corner Society* (1981), Erving Goffman's *Asylums* (1961), Ulf Hannerz's *Soulside* (1969) and Paul Willis' *Learning to Labour* (1977). Although the list could be longer, the number of studies of this calibre is still rather limited, considering the enormous number of social scientific works published every year. How can we explain this? The answer would seem to be simply that social psychology is hard to do. In some sense, social psychology involves developing what is so appropriately called an overall perspective. But what is meant by this?

Social psychology as a science and an art

The social psychology discussed in this book has gradually become an integrated part of sociology. But it is definitely not the case that all sociology is characterized by the perspective we call social psychology. If we are to develop this perspective, we must build on the tradition founded in Chicago and Frankfurt at the beginning of this century. What can we learn from this early development and how should we continue today?

A social psychological study must be marked by a great sensitivity for the whole. It involves painting a social and cultural landscape, and forming insights into the various social courses of events taking place in a specific location and during a special historical period. This demands a great deal of creativity. Thus, the best social psychological studies also have certain literary qualities. Their authors succeed in combining critical discussions and reflections on various concepts with the ability to give the reader insight into, and a feeling for, what has been studied. Such studies provide us with the tools to better understand and change the social reality in which we find ourselves.

Getting a handle on a complex social environment and forming an understanding of the processes at work there require theoretical flexibility. Researchers must be ready to use concepts from different scientific disciplines, to experiment with perspectives and analyses and to develop new ideas. The development of a critical approach to society is made possible by studying in detail how the social construction of various phenomena takes place. Garfinkel's ethnomethodological experiments have taught us how fragile and changeable social reality is and, at the same time, how tremendously strong people's resistance to change is. Social psychology takes place in the expanse between the stable and the changeable. The interest is not in describing social reality, but in developing a critical approach to it and in offering new knowledge.

Contemporary social psychology must be able to contribute to the development of a critical perspective on society and the individual. Thus, social psychology must be constantly updated in terms of analyses and concepts if it is to participate in contemporary analyses and contribute the specific knowledge of the relation between the individual and society that is its speciality. In such a social psychology, an empathetic approach is taken to the people studied, while the aim is also to expose oppression and injustice, and to dissect the conditions and structure of power. Thus, we have returned to the ambitions expressed at the beginning of the last century by the researchers in Chicago – ambitions we, at least in part, ought to hold on to as we have now entered into a new century.

In the first part of the book, I will present and critically deal with a number of important authors and traditions in social psychology. Many of the concepts and thoughts discussed in this part will also be used in Part II, where I will even discuss a few contemporary theoretical perspectives. Part II is intended to inspire the reader and show how social psychological thinking can be used to frame questions about, and analyse, various aspects of late-modern culture.

Selecting and presenting social psychological theories can, of course, be done in many different ways. It is often difficult to make distinctions, and we could, in principle, include all theories in which questions about the relationship between individual and society are framed. I have chosen to follow the development of the type of social psychology that was elaborated by authors such as Simmel and Goffman, and that is being further developed today by Giddens, Beck and other sociologists.

By isolating this variant of social psychological tradition, I am simultaneously disregarding a number of other theoretical approaches. I compensate for this, in part, by dealing more freely with various types of theory in the second part of the book. Naturally, this book should not be read as though it contained the only true version of today's social psychology. On the other hand, I think that the type of social psychology presented here is useful as a rough frame of reference for those engaged in empirical studies.

Simmel's attempt to formulate a critical social psychology at the beginning of the twentieth century is my point of departure. The development in twentieth-century Germany is then tied to the growth of the Chicago school. Both Simmel and the Chicago sociologists were fascinated by the changes taking place in the expanding big city milieu. They made shrewd observations of the transformations in people's living conditions in modern society. The analyses of big city life then bring us to Walter Benjamin and the influence of psychoanalytic theories on social psychology. I deal with Benjamin, Marcuse and Elias, among others. Later, we become acquainted with Goffman's analyses of the trivialities of everyday life. And finally, I discuss the possible death of social psychology and its incorporation into sociology. This becomes quite clear when we look at theoreticians such as Giddens, Bauman and Beck, who do not consider themselves to be social psychologists, but who, in spite of this, have much in common with the authors mentioned previously.

After an introduction to this particular mainstream social psychology, based within sociology, the reader should have good ground to stand on when later venturing into the broader spectrum of social psychologies. Before beginning to improvise, one should learn certain basics. Only then is it possible to work through and expand on those themes that constitute the focus of social psychology.

Notes

1 Translated by K.W. (Karen Williams).
2 Translated by K.W.
3 William McDougal (1908) and Edward Alsworth Ross (1908), respectively.
4 In this context we can mention *The Hobo*, by Nels Anderson (1923), *The Gang*, by Fredrick Trasher (1927), *The Marginal Man*, by Everett Stonequist (1937) and *The Slum and the Gold Coast*, by Harvey Warren Zorbaugh ([1929] 1978).

Part I Theoretical perspectives

Georg Simmel: the psychologist of social life

Objectivity and emotionality

Georg Simmel's work has long lain in the shadow of other sociological classics, but in the 1990s we can talk about a Simmel renaissance. Many of his papers have been published in English and have, thereby, been given greater exposure. At the beginning of the last century, the interpretation of Simmel's work that was influential in the USA emphasized his attempts to define and delimit *social forms*; thus, his attempts to analyse those distinctive features that characterize social institutions, social types and various kinds of social interaction (Simmel 1959). Now, Simmel has been rediscovered, and it is his analyses of modernity that are central. He is praised because early in his work he was able to capture and describe the vague, liquid and constantly changing processes that are often associated with the very meaning of the concept of modernity (Frisby 1981, 1992).

Whereas in his early work, and primarily in *The Philosophy of Money*, Simmel studies the differentiation of society and the process of individualization, much of his later work deals with how individuals, in various ways, manage the objectivization of the culture. Although his attitude towards people's potential to develop their individuality is positive, he simultaneously questions the concept of the individual. With time, he develops a theory of the human being that takes into account 'unconscious factors', irrationality, strong expressions of emotion and the fragmented nature of individuality. His later texts are marked by a great respect for people's private and inner lives, and for people's right to remain unexplained, subtle and secretive.

In order to understand Simmel's later analyses of people's emotional lives and his attempt to save subjectivity from a constantly growing and paralysing culture, we must compare his studies of the symbolic meanings of the money economy with his later analyses of love, shame, discretion, beauty, the face and so forth. It is only after studying the relationship between his two major sociological works – *The Philosophy of Money* and *Sociology* – that we can first begin to understand the cultural and philosophical existentialism he formulated in various texts towards the end of his life.

The Philosophy of Money was completed at the end of the nineteenth century, but published – significantly enough – in 1900. The work is extremely comprehensive, and covers everything from general cultural change to analyses of social characters and specific social problems. Although the title might seem to imply an economic theory, the work deals primarily with cultural change, social relationships and the prerequisites for real individuality. Simmel published his second major sociological work, *Sociology*, in 1908. Here we find analyses of social conflicts, power and poverty, as well as studies of how people, in various contexts, formulate their individual, distinctive characters.[1] In connection with this work, Simmel also published a number of shorter works in which he developed a sociological analysis of emotions.

In comparing these works and studying Simmel's analyses of love, discretion, secrets, lies and human passion, one is overwhelmed by the feeling of being present in, and experiencing, European cultural life during the early 1900s. We can study a discussion on individuality, choices and cultural production that anticipates and is largely similar to the discussion on postmodern culture being carried on today. Simmel contributes to the framing of these questions and shows how complex the question of human freedom and opportunities for self-fulfilment really is.

In order to comment on the consequences of the process of individualization, we must study the relationship between societal and cultural differentiation, on the one hand, and the individual's emotional reactions to these changes, on the other. Simmel stresses the fact that there is a difference between the generally increased occurrence of new lifestyles and possible identities, on the one hand, and the private individual's ability to take advantage of these new cultural conditions, on the other. Thus, cultural development does not automatically lead to greater individual freedom. Simmel also states that the increasing gap between the objective culture and individuals' subjective approach to this culture constitutes a growing problem.

In the following section, I will compare and contrast a number of Simmel's different lines of thought. I will also raise the question of where his analyses of the symbolic meaning of the money economy, social types, ways of reacting emotionally and the tragedy of culture actually lead us, and ask what consequences Simmel's sociology of culture has for contemporary analyses of the culture and the individual.

The money economy and the objective nature of life

It is difficult to read Simmel's *The Philosophy of Money* primarily as a work on economy or the historical development of the money economy. This work is, rather, a study of how social relationships and individuals are affected and transformed in a capitalistic society. Simmel shows how, in the wake of this societal development, a specific way of thinking and certain social types come into being. The money economy is marked by its objective nature – that is, money lacks individuality, peculiarity and character. Simmel writes: 'Money whose peculiarity lies in a lack of peculiarity' (Simmel [1900] 1990: 470). According to Simmel, human relationships tend, in the same way, to become more objective and to lose their specific and unique character:

> Money is not only the absolutely interchangeable object, each quantity of which can be replaced without distinction by any other; it is, so to speak, interchangeability personified.
>
> (Simmel [1900] 1990: 24)

The money economy has a number of paradoxical consequences for social relationships. On the one hand, people become interchangeable, alienated and develop ways of approaching one another that are impersonal. On the other hand, intimacy, freedom of choice and the possibility to satisfy various needs are facilitated. The real and symbolic power of money lies in its ability to liberate the individual from traditions and ties. Although Simmel highlights this aspect of freedom, he is also careful to point out and criticize the gradual objectivization of human relationships that is a consequence of the expansion of the capitalistic economy.[2]

The value of money, for some people, is supreme. Simmel's description of greed and extravagance captures the superficiality of this cult of money. Greedy people enjoy owning money. They collect and accumulate it without using it. Extravagant people, however, enjoy the very act of consumption – the moment when money changes hands. Thus, we have two social types representing two very different approaches to money. But, at the same time, these ideal types constitute the foundation of the capitalistic economy: accumulation of capital and consumption.

When these two forms of money worship are manifested in real, individual destinies, they take on a tragic character. He who is greedy can never enjoy life and things, but only the saving of money itself; this leads to material petrification. He who is extravagant lives only to experience the kick of consumption, but must continue the hunt for more of the same.

The money economy is the driving force behind a sweeping process of rationalization that contributes to the emergence of an objective culture: a culture to which the individual finds it more and more difficult to assimilate and develop a relationship. Thus, the increasing differentiation in society, which is a consequence of these processes, does not automatically lead to greater freedom in reality. Even if, for example, fashion is characterized by differentiation and constant change, this does not mean that the individual's autonomy is promoted, and it definitely does not mean that we can talk about individuality or *authenticity*.[3] The differentiation into different life-styles and expressions of style is a consequence of changes in what Simmel terms the objective culture. And, at the same time, the growth of this culture also constitutes a threat to the search for authenticity.

One consequence of the growth of the abstract culture and of the intellectualization of culture observed by Simmel is an increased distance between family members and between people in general. But this increased distance corresponds, in turn, to an increased closeness between people who earlier found themselves far apart. The money economy leads to decreased spatial and psychological distance between people, while it also creates a distance in the relationships between people. In other words, the relation between the local and the global has been drastically transformed during modernity.

More and more, human relationships are marked by the paradoxes and duality that characterize the capitalistic economy. We have both freedom and compulsion, distance and closeness, and a constant yearning to satisfy excessive desires. These paradoxes become most evident in big cities, where we find many different social relationships and mixtures of cultural styles.

The joys and sorrows of big city life

The Philosophy of Money is a story about modern society, but also about the big city and its people. To be sure, Simmel wrote his famous essay on the big cities and intellectual life in 1903, but his principal interpretation of big city life could already be found in his book from 1900. Even if *The Philosophy of Money* is largely a philosophical discourse on the symbolic meanings of the money economy, Simmel constantly returns to the effects of this economy on human relationships.

We encounter no tangible people in Simmel's texts, but rather temporarily embodied approaches to modernity. The social types we meet – the pauper, the adventurer, the stranger, the prostitute, the miser, the spendthrift and others – are expressions of both the advantages and disadvantages of modernity. Although Simmel's view of mankind's future becomes increasingly darker, I think we can learn to identify the ambivalences, paradoxes and nuances in his texts, and use them to highlight the complexity that characterized big cities in the early 1900s.

Simmel's stranger, who received his final *Gestalt* in *Sociology*, is already in place in Berlin in 1900. This figure is well suited to the impersonal, transitory and objective form of social relationships that is cultivated in the capitalistic money economy. The stranger has neither historical roots in the environment nor in the social relationships he is temporarily affected by, and he can, thus, develop a relatively objective approach to social reality. By developing a dissociated and rational approach to financial transactions and to people, the stranger embodies the principles that drive the modern capitalistic economy forward – an economy that is no longer about gifts and returned favours or about personal relationships, but instead about objective distance and means-end rationality.[4] Thus, Simmel's description of the stranger also constitutes an attempt to capture an essential dynamic in the capitalistic society:

> The significance of the stranger for the nature of money seems to me to be epitomized in miniature by the advice I once overheard: never have any financial dealings with two kinds of people – friends and enemies. In the first case, the indifferent objectivity of money transactions is in insurmountable conflict with the personal character of the relationship; in the other, the same condition provides a wide scope for hostile intentions which corresponds to the fact that our forms of law in a money economy are never precise enough to rule out wilful malice with certainty. The desirable party for financial transactions – in which, as it has been said quite correctly, business is business – is the person completely indifferent to us, engaged neither for us nor against us.
>
> (Simmel [1900] 1990: 227)

The stranger has no emotional ties to the people he does business with. This makes doing business easier. The stranger is able to profit by the principles that reign in the capitalistic economy.

In contrast to the stranger, the prostituted woman represents a victim of a society in which everything is objectivized and transformed into goods that can be bought and sold on a market. As opposed to a gift, which requires a counter-reaction and which is based on a human relationship, money is strictly objective in nature. That which can be bought is also reduced to being a piece of merchandise and a means. The objective character of money is well suited to a human economy that is focused on consumption of experiences and, in the worst case, also of people. By becoming a piece of merchandise, the prostitute is degraded and loses her human dignity. However, it is not only the prostitute who is negatively affected by this financial transaction, but also the client.

> Of all human relationships, prostitution is perhaps the most striking instance of mutual degradation to a mere means, and this may be the strongest and most fundamental factor that places prostitution in such a close historical relationship to the money economy, the economy of 'means' in the strictest sense.
>
> (Simmel [1900] 1990: 377)

The capitalistic economy leads to an upheaval of intimate relationships and of people's internal psychological approach to the surrounding world. Simmel describes two personal strategies that are increasingly common and that can be used to deal with the changes in the culture. The *cynic's* reaction to the tendency towards the levelling of values is perverse curiosity. The cynic makes sweeping generalizations over everyone and everything, and enjoys this reduction of feelings, values and experiences.

Another way to approach the same societal tendencies is to develop a *blasé attitude*. This attitude is a reaction to the increasing amount of stimuli and experiences offered by society. The constant search for a 'kick' and various kinds of experience results in recurrent disappointments. When the effect of the latest experience has dissipated, a feeling of emptiness takes its place. Thus, the bombardment of stimuli and the enormous assortment of experiences cause people to withdraw into themselves and develop an attitude of indifference towards life. The more people try to cure their indifference by finding new experiences and kicks, the faster this blasé attitude develops.

The money economy pulls all human relationships into its symbolic orbit. It colours everything from business transactions to intimate love relationship. The result of this economy is the growth of new forms of human relationship. These relationships still constitute expressions of trust, love, intimacy, joy and other feelings. But in a society that is becoming more and more abstract in character and in which social relationships are increasingly controlled through the money economy, the basic conditions for social relationships are in a state of change. These changes can lead to increased individual freedom, but also to petrified human relationships in which joy and desire have turned into a blasé or cynical and indifferent attitude towards life.

This possible freedom, however, must also be realized in some form of identity project. By this, Simmel means that an inner homelessness has developed. People lack a solid core, and tend to place more and more of their identity in external objects – in the world of things. The project of modern man would seem to be increasingly paradoxical. The remedies people seek for their rootlessness and cultural confusion do not lead to improvement, but instead intensify their feelings of fragmentation.

In 1911, Simmel published an essay entitled 'The Adventurer' (Simmel 1971). According to the reasoning found in *The Philosophy of Money*, this social type could be considered to be the most extreme consequence of the money economy. The adventurer lives exclusively in the present, cut off from the past as well as the future. He or she exists in a dream world and accepts this world's fluid and variable features. The adventurer is the standard-bearer of modernism. He or she does not hesitate to break all ties and devotes himself or herself to the unconditional exploration of life. Life's unpredictability and randomness feed the adventurer's fantasies and dreams of a better life.

Adventurers leave behind them all material ties and set off on a hazardous journey into the internal and external world. To the onlooker, their attitude towards life seems to include a touch of insanity, but taking chances and risks is an important part of their lifestyle. While adventurers can take advantage of the opportunities offered by a changeable culture, they also expose themselves to constant risks. They are always prepared to seize the moment, and are, in this way, able to adapt themselves to cultural changes. At the same time, however, they lack an inner psychological stability and are dependent on constant experiences.

The development of social types such as the miser, the spendthrift, the pauper, the prostitute, the stranger and the adventurer constitutes the most distinct manifestation of the capitalistic economy's influence on human interaction. Although Simmel wants to stress the negative effects of this social change, he is also careful to point out that it is possible for people to avoid and protect themselves from the very worst consequences of capitalism. People's ability to keep things secret, to be discreet and to never completely reveal who they are – *the strategy of constant escape* – is the most marked feature of the emotionology of modernity.

The emotionology of modernity

In his early papers and major work on the philosophy of the money economy, Simmel dedicated himself to outlining the overall changes in modernity. Later, however, in his sociological papers, Simmel focused on the individual and the sphere of intimacy. He was interested in the contradictory relation between society and individuals – between the whole and its parts. While the whole has a tendency to consist of its parts, it is the specific organization of the parts that determines the overall impression. Take, for example, the face:

> The face is the most remarkable aesthetic synthesis of the formal principles of symmetry and of individuality. As a whole, it realizes individualization; but it does so in the form of symmetry, which controls the relations among the parts.[5]
>
> (Simmel 1959: 279ff)

Simmel, in a later essay on the nature of philosophy, stresses even more strongly the contradiction between the parts and the whole[6] (Simmel 1959). This emphasis on the contradiction between the general and the individual became increasingly important to Simmel. Many people are still tackling these questions today, which is why we will take a closer look at the way in which Simmel conceptualizes this culture conflict.

Humans are extremely social beings. They are nourished by social life. However, this sociability can also lose its connection to everyday life and be transformed into a pure and lifeless social form. Simmel writes: 'If sociability entirely cuts its ties with the reality of life out of which it makes its own fabric (of however different a style), it ceases to be a play and becomes a desultory playing-around with empty forms, a lifeless schematism which is even proud of its lifelessness' (Simmel 1950: 56).

The cultural development that Simmel describes in his later papers constitutes a clear threat to this sociability. People must, therefore, develop a number of strategies in order to protect themselves from the overabundance of impressions and the objectivization of the culture that threaten individual creativity. In the big city, the individual develops a cynical and blasé attitude towards others and towards life in general. In order to protect himself from all these impressions and from the bombardment of stimuli and visual shocks that are produced in the big city, modern man tends to retreat to the sphere of intimacy. This retreat from 'modernity' is also one of modernity's central aspects. People are forced to develop strategies in order to maintain their self-esteem and identity. The purpose of these strategies is to make people more obscure. One way to deal with an external threat is to keep things secret:

> The secret puts a barrier between men but, at the same time, it creates the tempting challenge to break through it by gossip or confession – and this challenge accompanies its psychology like a constant overtone. The sociological significance of the secret, therefore, has its practical extent, its mode of realization, only in the individual's capacity or inclination to keep it to himself, in his resistance or weakness in the face of tempting betrayal.[7]
>
> (Simmel 1950: 334)

The secret constitutes a necessary psychological defence in a world that threatens to destroy individuality. By setting up a kind of barrier against the surrounding world – attempting to keep secrets and keeping unique experiences out of view – the individual can counteract the hypostasis that threatens all life.

The individual, by refusing to reveal his or her secrets, can protect his or her inner emotional life from being exploited by the subjectivity that is promoted in the capitalistic economy. In an essay on discretion, Simmel writes that if we take away the possibility for people to remain mysterious and secretive, we also take away their human dignity (Simmel 1950). In order to preserve their human dignity and their ability to attract others, people must develop the art of maintaining their integrity. According to Simmel, many love relationships have dissolved because the individuals have become much too visible for one another. In a culture that threatens to transform the sphere of intimacy and cultural creativity into lifeless social forms – devoid of all humanity – it is, as a matter of course, necessary to develop the ability to remain obscure and to defend the sphere of privacy at all costs.

Simmel's version of the emotionology of modernity deals largely with how individuals can preserve the right to formulate their own identity and how the abstract culture can be prevented from enveloping all forms of social interaction and intimate relations in an increasingly widespread alienation. By focusing on the unpredictable, obscure and unattainable, Simmel's goal is to show how we can safeguard individuality and the peculiarity that distinguishes humans. One of humankind's central driving forces is the constant longing to arrive at some kind of truth about life and about other people, but this search is a fatal one. We can never know another person completely, and it is precisely this impossibility that drives people to continue their search and that upholds their desire for the tacit. Love for another person is awakened and maintained by fascination with the prospect of the unknown and inaccessible. If anticipation and suspense cease to exist, the love relationship is also threatened.

In Simmel's later works, the question of the relation between individual and culture is transformed into a more philosophical discussion of the general and the specific in life. Simmel was to grapple with this complex of problems until his death in 1918.

Culture and existence

Simmel, in his later papers, first deals with objective versus subjective culture, and later deals with discussions of life versus form. Although these dualistic notions might seem similar, there are crucial differences between them (Nedelmann 1991).

The conflict between the objective and the subjective culture is about the difficulties people have with using the abstract culture and basing their lives on it. According to Simmel, we are surrounded by thousands of superfluous things that we are unable to free ourselves from. A cultural logic develops, and this logic has a life of its own. The relationship between the individual and the culture ceases to function, and this creates an unfathomable gap between subjective and objective culture. People withdraw in order to defend the last vestiges of their individuality, while the culture is objectivized and loses its aura (Simmel [1911] 1981).

When Simmel makes the transition to talking about life and form, his interest shifts from social life to a philosophical discussion of the conditions of life. What he calls life is a driving force that – like Freud's instinctual drives – is the basis for all human existence. Life and form are constantly involved in a dialectic interplay, but they are also one another's enemies. On the one hand, we have life; it flows and cannot be controlled; it is unpredictable and opposes all attempts to create structure and order. On the other hand, however, all types of human existence presuppose a form and structure. This social form threatens to kill life. But life always finds a way out. And so on, and so forth (Simmel 1971).

Although Simmel's linguistic usage is different towards the end of his life, he still constantly refers back to the same fundamental and irreconcilable conflict between some type of subjectivity or inner driving force, on the one hand, and the abstract culture or social forms, on the other. This conflict tends to create an increasingly wider gap between the individual and the culture:

> Life wishes here to obtain something which it cannot reach. It desires to transcend all forms and to appear in its naked immediacy. Yet the processes of thinking, wishing, and forming can only substitute one form for another. They can never replace the form as such by life which as such transcends the form. All these attacks against the forms of our culture, which align against them the forces of life 'in itself', embody the deepest internal contradictions of the spirit. Although this chronic conflict between form and life has become acute in many historical epochs, none but ours has revealed it so clearly as its basic theme.
>
> (Simmel 1971: 393)

Simmel wrote these lines during his last year of life. He expresses a pessimism about culture that is, in many ways, similar to the pessimism that Freud formulated in his book *Civilization and its Discontents* ([1930] 1986). Simmel had just lived through the First World War when he formulated his thoughts about life and form. Freud wrote his book on the struggle between life and death instincts during a troubled time in which the spectre of Fascism would soon begin its devastation of Europe. The struggle between life and death was intensified, and the great existential questions were brought to a head. The question is whether the pessimism about culture that thinkers such as Freud and Simmel stood for has anything to contribute to today's discussions.

A cul-de-sac of culture pessimism?

In both of Simmel's main works, we find interesting attempts to develop a social psychology for modern society. In his exciting essays and fragments of text on the stranger, the adventurer, the face, greed, extravagance, discretion, secrets and lies and so on, Simmel succeeds in capturing the subjective life of the individual and relating it to central changes in the culture. Now and then, Simmel provides us with brilliant analyses of the relation between psychological processes, social interaction and culture. His thoughts on nervous disorders typical of the period, big city life and the money economy's transformations are woven together so as to form an exciting social psychological fabric. The theory of the symbolic consequences of the money economy for human relationships is telling, and more specific reaction patterns and actions are made comprehensible by such an analysis.

The question is, however, whether or not this intellectual model of the tragedy of culture, which becomes clearer and clearer in Simmel's papers, leads us into a theoretical cul-de-sac. If we follow his intellectual development and try to understand how he relates to people and the culture, we become increasingly disappointed with his tendency to resort to stereotypes. Simmel's descriptions of modern culture become more and more clichéd, and his attempts to save individuality result in a worship of escapism, obscurity and the absolutely private life. It is difficult to completely accept Simmel's picture of an increasingly abstract and unapproachable culture and of an individual who – trying to save his or her individuality at all costs – retreats into the private world.

Why, then, do Simmel's social psychological analyses of modernity constitute such a mixture of brilliant observations and gross and simplistic generalizations? Philosophical concepts such as subjective and objective culture, life and form are made lifeless, and the use of these concepts leads to a view of social life that is quite lacking in variation and subtlety.

Analyses of the money economy's symbolic meanings play a central role in Simmel's thinking. Although the method of highlighting a specific driving force and systematically showing how it affects all social life is efficient, there is a risk that the analyses will become self-perpetuating, that is that everything is explained according to a supreme principle. Because of its symbolic status, the money economy influences everything from love relationships to consumption of goods. Thus, while this analysis gives us insights into how the capitalistic economy affects human relationships, nuances regarding power relations, politics, laws and collective action, for example, are left out. We run the great risk of exaggerating the symbolic influence that economic factors might have on social life. There are, obviously, other factors that shape the culture.

The question is, how fruitful is it to use analogies to analyse the relation between the money economy and human relationships? Such an approach presupposes a rather static relation between both of these levels of analysis. The advantage of using this type of reasoning is that it makes a discussion of the relation between greatly differing social processes possible. There are, however, also disadvantages. It is, for example, difficult to discern human relationships that are not directly affected by the capitalistic economy. This line of reasoning also tends to take on a much too abstract character. We miss the subtleties and diversity in social life.

It could be said that Simmel's social psychology has been fruitful primarily in terms of his analyses of social types and of the various strategies people develop to deal with the overflow of impressions and experiences to which they are exposed in the big city. Even if we do not accept the conclusions Simmel draws from his theoretical studies of culture, certain of his analytical devices are useful. I will conclude by presenting a few of the lines of thought that are still relevant to analyses of contemporary life.

Simmel distinguishes between *individualization* and *individuality*. Even if a greater diversity of cultural expressions and a differentiation of various lifestyles are developing in society, this development does not imply that private individuals are enriched and made more individual. If the distance between lifestyles and styles at the cultural level and the individual's activities becomes too great, both the culture and the individual are impoverished. Thus, individuals develop in their meeting with the culture. However, during periods in which such a genuine meeting is made difficult, individual development does not occur. Simmel considered his contemporary culture to represent such a period. The problem with Simmel's analysis is that he tends to objectivize both the culture and the individual, and both levels of analysis lack modulation. The culture is presented as being overly homogeneous, and the individual as totally fragmented and nearly dissolved. The dualistic notion on which these analyses are founded is problematic, in that it tends to lead us into a social psychological cul-de-sac, where culture and individual become separate categories and are no longer components in an analysis of social interaction.

The analysis of the emotionology of modernity that Simmel develops constitutes a good starting point for an exploration of how people react to various societal and cultural transformations. Whereas Simmel's focus is primarily on the defensive aspects of this emotionology – withdrawal into the private sphere and the will to preserve an aura around the personality – it is important to take this a step further and discuss the more offensive strategies and reactions belonging to the same emotionology. When Simmel analyses the social psychology of conflict, he certainly touches on these aspects – for example, when he highlights the positive and uniting function of aggression in human relationships. At the same time, however, he leaves out many of the other expressions of emotion that are used to shape the culture.

Simmel introduces the idea of the city as a *mental and symbolic space*. It is the very experience of the city itself that is central to many of Simmel's analyses. An important aspect of the city culture is the bombardment of stimuli and impressions experienced there. Lacking from Simmel's view of the city, however, are more specific analyses of the symbolic meanings associated with different areas and material objects. The strength of Simmel's work on the city lies in his analyses of the social relationships and social types that arise in this big city culture – a culture so strongly marked by the money economy.

By introducing colourful and dynamic *social types* such as the stranger, the adventurer and the miser, Simmel succeeds in saying something essential about modernity. These social types not only constitute individual manifestations, but they have even more general implications. The stranger's objective character, the adventurer's dream-like existence and the miser's money worship are all expressions of modernity. Through these analyses, Simmel is able to capture the connection between cultural change and the level of the actor, without reducing one level to the other. Although many of Simmel's concepts are too strongly tied to classic philosophical discourse – the limitations of which have been shown in many ways – there is still much to be derived from his analyses of the dynamics that characterize social interaction. His emphasis on paradoxes, oppositions and change has much to offer contemporary social psychology. The strength of his analyses lies in his attempts to formulate concepts that reconcile the relation between the cultural and individual levels of analysis. In this way, Simmel is sometimes able to capture essential aspects of modernity. At the same time, however, he sometimes pushes his analogies so far that they tend to turn into clichés and stereotypes. Although Simmel has commonly been criticized for his unsystematic studies of various phenomena and his lack of logic, I would like to claim just the opposite, that is, that he tends to push his systematics too far and is much too consistent in his attempts to hit the nail – of his contemporary culture and its problems – on the head.

Digression: Simmel and the Chicago school

Intellectual distance and creative proximity

Georg Simmel never travelled to Chicago, and for this reason we will never know what he would have thought about the city. However, several Chicago sociologists did go to Germany to participate in Simmel's seminars. Robert E. Park, who was one of the most influential sociologists in Chicago at the time, attended Simmel's seminars from 1899 to 1903 (Bulmer 1984). As a result of these visits, many of Simmel's articles were translated into English and published in *The American Journal of Sociology*. Thus, Simmel had a certain influence on the early intellectual development within the Chicago school. It is difficult to say, however, how great this influence was. Although many of the classic studies on Chicago's urban environment seem to have been influenced by Simmel's thinking, this is not always made clear in references to the literature. Without making any great claims about having reconstructed the relation between Simmel's ideas and the sociology that developed in Chicago, I will discuss a few similarities and differences between these two 'traditions'.

At the beginning of the 1900s, Chicago was experiencing steady growth and was a city with a very mixed population, both in terms of social class and ethnicity. Half of the city's 1.7 million residents were foreign-born. Lincoln Steffens (an American journalist) described the city as: '. . . first in violence, deepest in dirt; loud, lawless, unlovely, ill-smelling, new; an overgrown gawk of a village, the teeming tough among cities' (Bulmer 1984: 14). Given this description, we can readily understand why the sociologists in Chicago, led by Robert Park, had decided to regard the city as a large social laboratory, where one could study 'Life as it is lived'. Why travel to the North Pole or climb Mount Everest in order to find adventure when we have Chicago, argued Park (Lindner 1996: 31).

In the book *The City*, Park and Burgess formulated the foundations for the large-scale research programme on social and cultural life in Chicago that would later result in a number of interesting studies. The book not only included many essential questions about the city and its residents, but the authors also developed a specific theoretical approach. In addition to buildings, institutions and means of communication, they claimed that the city was also a mental space – a 'state of mind'. According to this view, we should approach the city as if it were a living organism, consisting of physical objects and geographical areas as well as people who try to shape their lives within the framework of a specific city environment. Through the study of how various neighbourhoods evolved, were populated, cultivated and changed, a human ecology was developed in Chicago.

Simmel's essay on the big cities and intellectual life had either a direct or an indirect influence on many of the research projects carried out in different areas of Chicago during the 1920s and 1930s. In contrast to Simmel, who was content to observe the city from a distance, the Chicago scientists were out in the city environment acquainting themselves with its neighbourhoods and people. This type of hands-on sociology was, thus, able to flesh out many of Simmel's concepts with more detailed and varied contents. Through these studies, we are even allowed to meet real people, and to study their view of the city.

Whereas Simmel's social types are theoretical constructions, the descriptions of the social types we meet in the Chicago studies, such as *The Hobo* or *The Marginal Man*, are based on people's own stories. Just as Simmel was able to show how, for example, the prostitute, the miser and the pauper developed in a specific time and were expressions of certain cultural and economic changes, the above studies give us a feeling for how these social types are formed by, and form, the culture. The different people we meet in studies such as *The Ghetto*, *The Hobo* and *The Gold Coast and the Slum* provide us with a living illustration of Chicago in the 1920s and 1930s. In these studies, people and milieux are merged together, creating intricate social and cultural networks.

Although Georg Simmel was not always included in the authors' list of references, he seems to have made his mark on Park and colleagues' successful research on big city culture in Chicago. We see Simmel's influence most clearly in notions about the city as a mental as opposed to an exclusively physical environment, in attempts to capture different social types and, lastly, in the use of the stranger as a kind of symbolic *Gestalt* for social change and modernity.

Two studies that provide us with a good illustration of the empirical work carried out in the Chicago school are Nels Anderson's *The Hobo* and Harvey

Zorbaugh's *The Gold Coast and the Slum*. *The Hobo* was the first study in the series of books produced within the framework of this school of thought, and *The Gold Coast and the Slum* was distinguished by its human ecological perspective on the transformations of the city environment.

The Hobo – the homeless adventurer

In a new edition of *The Hobo* ([1923] 1967), Nels Anderson explains the background to his classic study on homeless men. His story begins in 1882, when his father arrived in the USA, having emigrated from Sweden. Instead of establishing a permanent residence in the new country, Anderson's father travelled and took various temporary jobs. He worked as a farmer, logger, miner and so on. Anderson continued in his father's footsteps and took to the road, having neither a goal nor a direction. After several years of wandering, he finally settled in Chicago, where he began his studies in sociology. His interest in homeless men was shared by Robert Park, and the research project resulted in the now classic portrayal of the social situation for homeless men in Chicago during the 1920s.

In 1917, the number of homeless in Chicago varied between 30,000 and 70,000 individuals, depending on the fluctuations in the job market. For the most part, these men were on their way to a new job somewhere in the country, but when they needed to rest or to look for new work, they returned to the city. They lived in a specific area called *Hobohemia*. This area was completely dominated by men, and here we could find beggars, adventurers, gamblers, drug dealers and petty thieves. All of these men were homeless, but they came from different backgrounds and therefore differed in their ability to manage a life of itinerancy and insecurity. On the street and in the various camps where the homeless found temporary sanctuary, a strong sense of solidarity developed; but lawlessness also existed. One social type who sneaked around in these areas was the petty thief – *the Jack roller*. He robbed men while they were drunk and when they were sleeping. On the occasions when a petty thief was caught, he was in a grave situation and could even be beaten to death.

These men had various reasons for taking to the road in search of happiness. One factor was the instability of the job market, which forced individuals to look for temporary work and contributed to the precarious lifestyle. Many men were also drawn to the road in search of adventure. Anderson described this longing as a *wanderlust*:

> Wanderlust is a longing for a new experience. It is the yearning to see new places, to feel the thrill of new sensations, to encounter new situations, and to know the freedom and the exhilaration of being a stranger. . . . Tramp life is an invitation to a career of varied experiences and adventures. All this is a promise and a challenge. A promise that

all the wishes that disturb him shall be fulfilled and a challenge to leave the work-a-day world that he is bound to.

(Anderson [1923] 1967: 82)

Anderson makes a distinction between this type of adventurer (*the hobo*), who is a special type of homeless man, and other types such as the tramp, the seasonal worker, the alcoholic and those men who are permanent residents of Hobohemia. In one extract from the book, these types are described as follows: 'The hobo works and wanders, the tramp dreams and wanders and the bum drinks and wanders'.

The homeless men in Chicago were, in other words, a heterogeneous group of people with different fortunes. Although most of these men lived on a day-to-day basis, it was common for them to organize themselves in various ways. A kind of 'public sector for the homeless' developed that, among other things, consisted of union groups, religious movements, intellectual activities and training programmes. The homeless were known for reading the daily newspapers. At that time, there were a number of radical papers directed at the working class, and even a paper called *The Hobo* that dealt with the situation of the homeless more specifically. Thus, a particular culture was created in Hobohemia, which included a large selection of newspapers and magazines, authors, poets and intellectuals.

During the 1920s and 1930s, a tradition of authorship was developed among the homeless men. They depicted life as it was lived by the Chicago homeless on the road and in the streets. The following poem by Charles Thornburn was printed in *The Hobo News* in August 1921:

With ever restless tread, they come and go,
Or lean intent against the grimy wall,
These men whom fate has battered to and fro,
In the grim game of life, from which they all
Have found so much of that which is unkind,
Still hoping on, that fortune yet may mend,
With sullen stare, and features hard and lined,
They wander off to nowhere, and the end.

Their thoughts we may not fathom, in their eyes
One seems to sense a vision, as though fate
Had let one little glimpse of fairer skies
Brighten their souls before she closed the gate.
Yet have they hopes and dreams which bring them peace,
Adding to life's flat liquor just the blend
Called courage, that their efforts may not cease
To seek the gold, hid at the rainbow's end.

The poetry created by the homeless can be described as a mixture of realistic portrayals of their often difficult and vulnerable lives and a romantic love of wandering and adventure. Becoming involved in the culture that developed in Hobohemia often meant salvation from the destitution that characterized the life of the homeless; it was a way to create meaning in life.

Anderson provides a rich illustration of Chicago's homeless men at the beginning of this century. His reasoning about 'The hobo' as an adventurer would almost seem to be an empirical investigation of Simmel's social type. But Anderson never refers explicitly to Simmel. In *The Hobo* we become acquainted with the city milieux that the homeless see as their own territories. Individual human fates emerge against the background of historical change in the job market, the city and the public sector. As opposed to Simmel's more pessimistic depiction of modern culture, Anderson gives a varied and empathetic description of the people who populate the city.

The Gold Coast and the Slum

The strength of studies of the big city from the Chicago school lies in the combination of careful ethnographical investigations of different human fates and social types, on the one hand, and mappings of how various districts and subcultures develop in relation to one another, on the other. One study of the latter type is Harvey Zorbaugh's *The Gold Coast and the Slum* (Zorbaugh [1929] 1978).

Zorbaugh takes us with him on a wander through the city's different neighbourhoods and streets. According to Zorbaugh, one can read the city streets in the same way that one reads the strata on a boulder. Different areas have derived their character through the social groups that have populated them. Thieves, bohemians, leftist radicals, immigrants and various unsuccessful characters have found their home in the slum. These people are there for different reasons. Some are there because it is inexpensive to live there, and others because they are attracted to the people who populate the slum and to the environment itself.

In the same geographical area, distinctions are created between different groups. Such demarcation lines can originate from ethnicity, class and a number of other factors. About 30 different nationalities meet in the slum. They bring with them, and develop, different lifestyles, traditions and habits, which later come to characterize those areas of the city where these immigrants establish themselves. Within these different subcultures, a sense of collective solidarity develops, but this cultural pluralism leads, at the same time, to a fragmentation of the city and to conflicts between the various social groups. Zorbaugh writes:

> Yet its streets, teeming with life, thronging with strange people, resounding with outlandish tongues, and the noises of industry and commerce, are pervaded with the glamor and romance of the forward march of the greater city. This glamor and romance, however, exists in

the social distances that, while they make the city a mosaic of little cultural worlds intriguing to the journalist, the artist and the adventurer,
make it impossible for these same little worlds to comprehend one
another, and so atomize the life of the city.

(Zorbaugh [1929] 1978: 45)

Not far from the slum, we find a district called the Gold Coast. Although
only a stone's throw from the slum in geographical terms, on entering the
district we suddenly experience a completely different cultural milieu. On
the Gold Coast – where the *nouveaux riches* and more well-to-do people
live – the living conditions are in stark contrast to those in the slum. Life
here is all about knowing the right people, buying the right clothes, living
in the right neighbourhood and so on and so forth. This social game is
played using various, subtle status markers. For certain people, this symbolic game becomes a full-time activity:

> One of Chicago's wealthiest 'married maidens' has, for example, a
> calling list of two thousand names, filling two indexes, which contain
> merely the names of those to whom she owes obligations, or with
> whom she must keep in touch to keep in the game. She has to have a
> secretary to handle her correspondence, to plan her dances and recep-
> tions, to send out invitations, acknowledge other invitations, and keep
> track of her social obligations.
>
> (Zorbaugh [1929] 1978: 55)

The rich live on the Gold Coast. These people are extreme individualists.
They have no contact whatsoever with the people living in the slum, except
on those occasions when someone decides to pursue some form of charity
work.

Not far from the Gold Coast's fashionable district, we find a neighbourhood populated by people who, for some reason, spend a few years in the
city. Zorbaugh calls this part of the city 'The world of furnished rooms'. For
the most part, the people living here belong to the lower, white middle class.
These are people who either study or work, and who are in a reasonable
financial situation. According to Zorbaugh, it is these types of people who
increasingly leave their mark on the city. They spend some time there, and
then move on to the next destination. Their lives are characterized by temporary work and relationships. They are nomads without any real goal. This
type of individualization counteracts all forms of collective solidarity.

The solidarity and feelings of community that developed in certain parts
of the city became more and more threatened by a way of life that puts the
individual first and that is based on temporariness. According to Zorbaugh,
this lifestyle, which was first developed by bohemians and intellectuals,
affected increasing numbers of people. This resulted in a gradual disintegration of the social safety net and collective solidarity that had been built

up in certain city districts. The rapid development of the city divided the family and led to detraditionalization. The father's occupation was no longer handed down to the son, and the absence of role models in the local environment led to gang formation and criminality. To some extent, this development depended on the hybridization that occurred in the multicultural city:

> Cultures lose much of their identity. The mores tend to lose their sanctions. And in this cosmopolitan world, by virtue of this tolerance of the 'foreign' and interpretation of customs, traditional social definitions lose their meaning, and traditional controls break down. Groups tend to lose their identity, and the social patterns of these groups tend to merge into a hybrid something that is neither Sicilian nor Persian nor Polish, but of the slum.
>
> (Zorbaugh [1929] 1978: 152)

Although Zorbaugh did not regard this development as particularly positive, but instead as a threat to social ties and to the family as a creator of norms, it led to a subsequent development of the picture of the city and to changed relationships between people. Zorbaugh's ideas on hybridization, individualization and alienation can be interpreted as a further development of Simmel's theory of the big city. However, from the study of Chicago's city population, we get a deeper insight into how the interaction between various social groups develops and into the consequences of this development for the city.

From philosophy to journalism

It is obvious that Simmel had a great effect on the type of sociology that developed in Chicago at the beginning of the twentieth century. However, it is more difficult to deduce the exact nature of this influence. The studies of the big city that were carried out by people such as Wirth, Anderson, Zorbaugh and Stonequist, among others, in many ways give us a more varied picture of the city than we are given in Simmel's texts. But it is precisely Simmel's notions about the big city as a mental space, populated by a number of social types, that give structure to the ethnographical studies in Chicago's city environment. And the interactionistic perspective, especially, allows us to understand how the relation between different social groups affected the shaping of the city culture.

Whereas Simmel's increasingly philosophical interpretation of the city and its people – and of form and life – results in a pessimistic view of whether it is possible to live a good life in the modern urban milieu, the Chicago sociologists take as their starting point the innumerable variations that characterize the urban environment. Here, we find both destitution and unlimited opportunities for experimenting with lifestyles and relationships. Even if many of the analyses point out the negative consequences of the dissolution of traditional structures and the related individualization, we are given the chance to form our own opinion about the processes of change that are described.

Although the same type of criticism of civilization is present both in Simmel's studies of the urban and modern and in those coming out of the Chicago school, there is a difference in approach – one being distant and the other proximate. Simmel's analyses are marked by intellectual distance from the object of study, whereas, for example, Anderson's loving descriptions of homeless men in Chicago reveal a closeness to the people he meets. Simmel also chooses to use social types rather than concrete descriptions of people's lives.

If we read the studies from the Chicago school as a further development of, and variation on, certain of Simmel's ideas, we find that they also function as a bridge to Benjamin's Passage work in Paris, as well as to Goffman's dramaturgical analyses of people's attempts to adapt to the constant changes that characterize the big city and modernity.

Notes

1 Simmel does not explicitly use the notion of identity, but some type of identity concept can be construed from the content of many of his arguments.
2 Simmel is clearly influenced by Marx's discussion of alienation and reification, but does not relate this discussion to the issue of class in the same way that Marx does.
3 Simmel does not use the concept authenticity, which involves some form of genuineness on the part of the individual. However, my interpretation is that this concept is similar to Simmel's descriptions of sociality and 'authentic' individuality.
4 Simmel's ideas are similar to Max Weber's theory on the puritanical character, but also include the notion of consumption as an important mechanism in the capitalistic economy.
5 From Simmel's essay 'The Aesthetic Significance of the Face', from 1901; in Simmel (1959: 279ff).
6 'The Nature of Philosophy', in Simmel (1959: 309). Simmel writes: 'Thus the structure of metaphysical universals is explained: they do not hold for the very particulars of which they seem to be generalizations.'
7 Essay from 1906.

2 Psychoanalysis and social psychology

Dreamtime and the time of the body

At the end of the 1800s, the European landscape underwent drastic changes. Rural areas were depopulated and the cities were filled with people in search of a new life. While social scientists' interests were focused on these socio-material changes, an interest in the *inner world* was also on the rise. From a dissertation published in 1899 – the title of which included the year 1900 – we learn that dreams reveal our innermost, secret desires. In dreams, fragments of reality are used to falsify reality. Dreams do not reveal the world as it is, but as we would like it to be. But, by letting our innermost desires and longings come to the fore, dreams also contain an 'element of truth'. The book in question is Sigmund Freud's epoch-making work *The Interpretation of Dreams*. At the end of this we find the following prophetic lines:

> And the value of dreams for giving us knowledge of the future? There is of course no question of that. It would be truer to say instead that they give us knowledge of the past. For dreams are derived from the past in every sense. Nevertheless the ancient belief that dreams foretell the future is not wholly devoid of truth. By picturing our wishes as fulfilled, dreams are after all leading us into the future. But this future, which the dreamer pictures as the present, has been moulded by his indestructible wish into a perfect likeness of the past.
>
> (Freud [1900] 1985: 783)

The Interpretation of Dreams is a study of the symbolic language of dreams and the structure of human desire. By mapping the 'logic' of the inner world – and the constantly changing processes that characterize it – Freud provides us with analytical tools that can be used to understand the internal as well as the external world. The conflict between desires and the inert forces that counteract them takes place not only in the inner world, but even in the external, social world. Thus, the analysis model developed by Freud in *The Interpretation of Dreams* can also be used in attempts to understand processes in our social reality and in the culture. When Walter Benjamin – one of Freud's contemporaries – formulated his unfinished work on the dream worlds of Paris, he was obviously inspired by psychoanalysis. Psychoanalytic theory, however, would be used not only to understand consumption and transformations in material reality, but also to study changed attitudes towards the body and human sexuality.

Freud's psychoanalytic theory contained many building blocks, but one of the most important was his studies of human sexuality. Although we can, today, find reason to criticize many of Freud's more prescriptive statements and his views on masculinity and femininity, the fact remains that Freud was among the first theorists to demonstrate the plastic nature of human sexuality and instincts. Instincts and desires can be directed towards various objects and expressed in numerous different ways. Neither the nature of gender nor of sexuality is laid down in our genes, although – according to Freud – they are partly determined by hereditary preconditions. The individual's specific sexual preferences and instinctual structure develop in an interplay between the psychological and the social world.

By not tying sexuality and gender development to certain, given premises a priori, Freud opened up a discussion of different types of sexuality, and made it possible to carry out analyses of bodily sensations and experiences based on a psychological theory of the individual and his or her environment. The notion that sexuality and instincts are formed and pass through different stages – Freud talks about oral, anal and phallic development – has inspired many social scientists to study historical development in a similar way.

In 1939 – the year of Freud's death in London after a long-term illness – Norbert Elias' theory on the process of civilization was printed. This theory was based largely on Freud's ideas about the plastic character of instincts. Elias tied psychoanalytic ideas on the development of the superego, and the various psychosexual stages of development, to thoughts about the disciplinization of humankind and the growth of the state and the nation. These thoughts were close to those formulated by Freud in what was perhaps his most central work, *Totem and Taboo*. With his point of departure in culture theory, it was here that Freud founded his ideas about the incest taboo and 'The law of the Father'.

Towards the end of the 1800s, during his self-analysis, Freud had already begun to formulate rudimentary ideas about the importance of the Oedipus myth for human intellectual life. But the concept was developed, along with the constant stream of new ideas being added to the psychoanalytical frame of reference. The Oedipus complex theory dealt with the significant triangular drama that was taking place in the middle-class, nuclear family – a drama that focused on the child's sexuality, incestuous desires, shame, guilt and other strong feelings. What was primarily focused on, however, was not the social relationships existing between parents and children, but the psychological drama being enacted in the inner world. The nearly unlimited possibilities provided by the unconscious – for playing with various alternative scenarios and deeds – indicated a large number of possible developments of and solutions to this drama.

Although Freud certainly recommends a solution of the drama in which people abandon and sublimate their early and 'primitive' sexual desires and perversions, it is not at all obvious that this solution implies the greatest possible happiness. Freud's normative ideas about mature sexuality – in which the phallus and the heterosexual relationship are given supreme importance – were greatly criticized in connection with the growth of feminist criticism and the further development of psychoanalysis. But this type of criticism against Freud's idea of the importance of the symbolic father was first made by, and constituted a point of departure for, those who purported critical theory and tried to combine radical social thought with psychoanalysis. Herbert Marcuse's work *Eros and Civilization* (1955) was an early attempt to relativize the notion of the Oedipus complex's normative aspects. Later, this project would be developed further by various feminists.

During the 1930s and afterwards, countless attempts were made to combine psychoanalysis and social theory. Those who tried to apply psychoanalytical concepts directly to society were often unable to formulate dynamic theories. The result of these attempts was a fruitless psychologization of society rather than the development of a critical social theory. However, many of the attempts made during the 1930s – the same decade in which Freud wrote his most famous work – have continued to serve as examples of how psychoanalytic theory can inspire us in our search for social psychological models. All of the theoreticians discussed in this chapter have, in one way or another, been tied to the Frankfurt school. The Institut für Sozialforschung (the Institute for Social Research) was a meeting place for the most exciting culture theoreticians and social psychologists of the time.

In the following presentation, I will concentrate on three influential theoreticians: Walter Benjamin, Norbert Elias and Herbert Marcuse. They will serve as landmarks for different approaches to the application of psychoanalytical thought in the social sciences. I will *not* deal with the Frankfurt school's different attempts to analyse the authoritarian character and Fascism. This has already been touched on in the introduction to the book, and several sources are provided for the interested reader. Instead, I have chosen to focus on three different lines of thought developed in psychoanalytically oriented social psychology. These themes will be elaborated further in the thematic parts of the book, where I will return to Benjamin, Elias and Marcuse.

Walter Benjamin's dream passages

In Benjamin's (1950) work *Berliner Kindheit um neunzehnhundert* the child's view and world of experiences are central. In contrast to Marcel Proust, whose interest was exclusively in the past, Benjamin was interested in the dialectics existing between the past, present and future. Benjamin tried to understand the contemporary world through the awake and partially unspoiled eyes of the child. Children stand on the threshold between the paradise that is childhood existence and the reality of adult life. Children's language and their ability to look at things without preconceived notions have yet to be ruined. By looking through the eyes of a child, we can win back the symbolic meaning that is constantly threatened in a middle-class, capitalistic society:

> The child's creative perception of the objects in fact recollects the historical moment when the new technology was first conceived – that 'too-early' epoch when, onto a new nature still in the stage of myth, all kinds of archaic symbols were cathected. The difference is that now the technical aspects of that nature have matured historically. Over the century, they have become 'merely new', displaying only their 'modern' or 'dashing' side. But: 'The child can in fact do something of which the adult is totally incapable: "discover the new anew"'. This discovery reinvests the objects with symbolic meaning and thus rescues for the collective memory their utopian signification.
>
> (Buck-Morss 1993: 274)

The desire to preserve the ability to have 'living' experiences is a main thread throughout Benjamin's publications. The transition from *Erfahrung* to *Erlebnis*, that is, from unconscious fragments of memory to conscious, constructed memory, always implies a loss of meaning. To denominate an object – to give it a name – is also to reduce its importance and lose something of the experience of the original meeting with the object.

If we are to understand the present or the Utopias that are formulated at a given moment, we must study the dialectics existing between the past – its rituals, mythical ideas and experiences – and the poetics and dream images of the present. By wandering the streets of Paris and drinking in its historically charged atmosphere, Benjamin attempted to capture the processes of change that, in his opinion, would soon result in a total transformation of society:

> The street takes the flâneur back to bygone days. It leads him downwards, if not to the mothers still into the past, which is all the more

spellbinding because it is not his own private past. All the same, this past is always a childhood time. But why should it be his own past? When he walks upon the asphalt, his steps have a remarkable resonance. The gaslight shining down on the paving-stones casts an ambiguous light upon this complex ground.[1]

(Benjamin 1992: 344)

Just as Freud tried to understand the subtleties of longing and the dream's distortion of human desire, Benjamin also studied his contemporary dream worlds and traced the possible Utopias and desires expressed in them. During his wanderings through Paris, Benjamin focused on the changes in middle-class culture and capitalism that he thought he could read in phenomena such as the department stores, arcades, architecture, fashion and prostitution of the time. What he thought he observed was a capitalism that was increasingly losing its legitimacy and gradually becoming eroded.

The Utopian desires that perhaps could be traced in the city took on a more and more perverse character; that is, they were distorted to the point of unrecognizability, and petrified. The decay and fragmentation found by Benjamin during his wanderings are expressed most strongly in the figure of the prostitute. In a harder social climate, more and more people were forced to 'prostitute themselves' – to sell their bodies and their manpower: 'Under the sign of unemployment, the intended advance moved forward with large steps; the *keep smiling* of the labor market takes from the love market the whore's inviting smile'[2] (Benjamin 1992: 292, original emphasis).

The figures we meet in Benjamin's Paris – the collector, the *flâneur* and the prostitute – are people living on the edge. They represent different aspects of capitalism and the self-destruction that threatens this social order. The collector attempts to save objects from destruction and to preserve something of the aura surrounding them. The *flâneur* finds himself in the middle of modernity's whirlpool. He throws himself headlong into the intoxication he finds in the crowd and in his own aimless search for something he cannot define. And the prostitute is the ultimate sign of the most extreme consequence of capitalism – the objectivization of humans. We are never told what will happen after the death of capitalism. Benjamin tries to trace the origins of desire and its path of development, but he wanders away on the streets of Paris and gets lost. But even though capitalism is still going strong and the arcades of Paris have been replaced by modern, global department store chains, Benjamin's vision – of how the representations of the past, present and future are mixed and create dialectical representations that are difficult to interpret – is still a powerful mental image. One question raised by Benjamin is how unconscious desires are to survive in a culture that is characterized by increasing transparency and demystification. The question is whether the loss of the aura also implies the loss of the energy that flows out of the unconscious.

The optical unconscious

The existence of photographs and films makes it possible to approach human beings in an entirely new way. That which has earlier been hidden – not observable by the naked eye – now appears very clearly in, for example, the photograph. But this penetration and this loss of the aura of art are irrelevant if they do not lead to a constructive calling into question of the existing society. A photograph that does not help to reveal social oppression – but instead exalts consumption – becomes a fetish; it is a sign of the crisis in which society finds itself and of the inability to solve the conflicts that characterize this crisis.

The medium of film, to an even greater degree, allows us to see a reality that is otherwise hidden under layers of mystifications; mystifications built up by humans who have a limited capacity to see things as they really are. But the use of such a powerful tool brings with it a great responsibility in terms of how the film-maker chooses to approach and interpret social reality. Simply detaching objects from their context and exposing them is not very constructive. The film camera gives us access to the unconscious, but the question is, how should we use this knowledge?

> The act of reaching for a lighter or a spoon is familiar routine, yet we hardly know what really goes on between the hand and metal, not to mention how this fluctuates with our moods. Here the camera intervenes with the resources of its lowerings and liftings, its interruptions and isolations, its extensions and accelerations, its enlargements and reductions. The camera introduces us to unconscious optics as does psychoanalysis to unconscious impulses.
>
> (Benjamin 1992: 230)

According to Benjamin, tradition and rituals – the roots of art – have been replaced by politics. Because film allows us to see the mechanisms of coercion that control our existence and the self-built prisons in which we live, it also creates the possibility of liberation. If the artistic and scientific uses of film can be combined, its revolutionary function will also be enabled.

Just as psychoanalytical knowledge about the unconscious can be used to liberate people, film can provide us with knowledge that can be used to expose oppression and mechanisms of coercion. In Benjamin's work, we find a politicized unconscious, located in the city's dream worlds and in the media. Access to the unconscious creates increasingly better conditions for detailed analyses of the mechanisms that counteract emancipation from political oppression. But Benjamin's analyses of these forces do not include any details or recommendations about the final shape of this good society.

While Benjamin brought the Utopian forces of dreams into focus, Norbert Elias concentrated on the widespread bodily discipline and suppression of desire that were, in his opinion, the result of specific societal changes.

The plasticity of instinct control

The year 1939 – the same year that Elias published his major work on the process of civilization – marked the beginning of the Second World War. This was one of the reasons that Elias' work did not receive the attention it deserved until the 1970s. When Elias formulated his theory he would, in all likelihood, have had access to most of Freud's publications. However, in spite of the fact that Elias' work is obviously influenced by Freud's psychoanalytical theory, references to Freud are few. Elias is careful to distance himself from the non-historical features of psychoanalysis. His project is an attempt to apply the psychoanalytical theory of development to historical change and theory.

Elias' basic idea is that sociogenesis mirrors psychogenesis. According to Elias, the development described by Freud, in which the superego tends to suppress various libidinous and aggressive instinctual impulses – thereby exerting inner control over desire – has taken on different qualities during different historical epochs. His basic thesis is that a modern, differentiated society in which the interplay between people becomes more and more complicated also presupposes a high degree of internal control over instincts and desires. The fear of physical and external punishment is successively replaced by anxiety and feelings of guilt towards the superego – the authority responsible for internal punishment. Just as the superego has an inner monopoly on psychological violence and regulates people's instincts, the growth of the nation-state implies a monopoly on violence and a prohibition of uncontrolled physical violence.

However, just as the monopoly of state violence can change and be demolished, inner control and the command of instincts can also be gradually dissolved. Thus, it is the fear of potential physical violence that results in the creation of more and more complicated adjustments of external behaviour and the internal psychological life. A 'civilized' person need no longer be subject to external social control. He has self-control over his aggression and his need for acting out feelings and instincts. But the balance between the external and the internal is weak. If the relations between different social groups change and if the state is weakened, even people's degree of self-control will be affected. Thus, what Elias outlines is the dynamic relation between sociogenesis and psychogenesis.

Just as increasing portions of the psyche are subject to the discipline of the superego, more and more social groups are enveloped in the process that leads to increased societal control of instincts. For example, Elias shows how members of the royal court were among the first to discipline their emotional lives, and how this psychological approach then spread to the middle class, and finally to the working class. Over time, this disciplinary process characterized increasing numbers of social groups until, finally, the entire society was involved in this process of change.

The analogy between the state and the superego is a striking one, but the question is whether it holds under critical observation. In Freudian theory, the superego is a more complex phenomenon than is suggested by Elias' use of the concept. An overly dominant superego can cause melancholy and other types of psychological disturbance. In other words, a tyrannical superego can threaten an individual's entire existence. Elias does not consider this problem. He almost entirely avoids the question of what happens when the control of instincts becomes too strong.

In studying the arrangement of Elias' analyses, one might suspect that he has followed the psychoanalytic stages of psychosexual development step by step. His point of departure – in his analyses of how instincts and bodily excretions are formed during a historical process – is the idea of the oral, anal and phallic stages. We are told that humans have learned to suppress their need to, among other now offensive behaviours, belch, fart and expose their genitals. Rules for how one should behave in public are given in various books on etiquette. As we approach modern times, these rules become stricter and stricter. In a passage from the first part of the theory of civilization, we are given insight into things such as how people viewed the sounds of flatulence (Elias [1939] 1989). The following specifications are taken from Erasmus' book *De civilitate morum puerilium* from 1530:

> To contract an illness: Listen to the old maxim about the sound of the wind. If it can be purged without a noise that is best. But it is better that it be emitted with a noise than that it be held back. . . . Even though he had to be careful not to fart explosively in the holy place, he nevertheless prayed to Zeus, though with compressed buttocks. The sound of farting, especially of those who stand on elevated ground, is horrible. One should make sacrifices with the buttocks firmly pressed together.
>
> (Elias [1939] 1989: 130)

Elias' presentation allows us to follow how the body has been disciplined and how people have put more distance from everything that ties them to their 'bestial past'. But the question of the relation between sexuality and aggression is never systematically addressed. Elias' main focus is on the regulation of social violence. In modern society, open physical violence is forbidden. The state's monopoly on violence, together with greater self-control over violent impulses, has led to the development of various arenas where people can practise lawful violence. Perhaps the best example of such an arena is sports (Elias and Dunning 1986). While watching a soccer game, spectators can channel and release some of their aggressive impulses.

In Elias' work, we find a strong tendency to frame questions about and discuss the mechanisms of violence, but the question is: how should we conceive the connection between suppression of violence and repression of sexuality? Elias never develops any ideas about what constitutes a good society. To what end, then, is all this self-discipline? Will we become happier human beings or is there a risk that we will lose all contact with our inner 'bestial' instincts? The closest Elias comes to Utopia is in the last few lines of his second book about the process of civilization:

> Only with the tensions and conflicts between men can those within men become milder and less damaging to their chances of enjoyment. Then it need no longer be the exception, then it may even be the rule that an individual person can attain the optimal balance between his imperative drives claiming satisfaction and fulfilment and the constraints imposed upon them (and without which man would remain a brutish animal and a danger as much to himself as to others) – that condition to which one so often refers with big words such as 'happiness' and 'freedom': a more durable balance, a better attunement, between the overall demands of man's social existence on the one hand, and his personal needs and inclinations on the other.
>
> (Elias [1939] 1982: 333)

In his attempts to study the relation between the individual's psychological life and the development of more comprehensive structures, Elias sometimes misses the nuances and complexity that otherwise mark psychoanalytical concepts. Whereas Elias uses a concept of the superego that only implies various degrees of self-control, within psychoanalysis the notion is used to indicate everything from the establishment of certain ego ideals to the superego's role as a punishment authority that threatens to suffocate and destroy the personality. Neither does Elias touch on the close relation between life and death instincts. This set of problems is more thoroughly investigated by Herbert Marcuse.

The law of the Father: on this side of Oedipus and beyond

Discussions about the increased undermining of the institution of patriarchy and its consequences had already begun in the studies of the authoritarian personality. The basic idea and point of departure was that the father was becoming more and more marginalized in the family and that his authority was in question – only to be replaced by other external forms of authority. An especially important topic was the negative effects of the mass media on the family. In early analyses, the diminution of patriarchal authority was considered to be alarming. It was thought that there was a danger in replacing the father's more benign authority with other authoritarian forces. Such an analysis was certainly influenced by, among other things, Freud's *Totem and Taboo* from 1913. The murder of the proto-father resulted in the clan of brothers establishing a power that was based on the symbolic father. And this father figure was much stricter and more punishing than the proto-father. Thus, the weakening of the middle-class father's real power led to the emergence of Fascism's father figure and to the totalitarian society. But five years after the second study on the authoritarian personality was published in the USA, Herbert Marcuse wrote his book *Eros and Civilization* (1955). In this book, an entirely different view of the importance of the symbolic father for the creation of culture was presented.

In his Utopia – where it was no longer necessary for society to be based on oppression and the extraction from the worker of all he or she can give – Marcuse predicted the Eros revolution that would later be manifested in various ways in the USA. And in his total affirmation of a sexuality that was not exclusively based on genitally oriented desires, but that included the entire body, Marcuse anticipated feminist discussions on the body and sexuality. According to Marcuse's analyses, the father's authority and the patriarchal system were associated with ruthless exploitation of nature and human beings. As the antithesis to this system, he proposed a societal system in which this type of oppression – which is associated with capitalism – would be stopped. As a consequence of continued technological development, he proposed that it should be increasingly possible for people to enthusiastically and pleasurably shape their work and leisure time. Thus, the affirmation of forces such as these and of people's longing to fill their lives with meaning and pleasure implies a threat to capitalism. Oedipus – who in Marcuse's version of psychoanalysis symbolizes the patriarchal and oppressive capitalistic system – is presented in contrast to the mythical and literary figures Orpheus and Narcissus:

> The images of Orpheus and Narcissus reconcile Eros and Thanatos. They recall the experience of a world that is not to be mastered and controlled but to be liberated – a freedom that will release the powers of Eros now bound in the repressed and petrified forms of man and nature. These powers are conceived not as destruction but as peace, not as terror but as beauty. It is sufficient to enumerate the assembled images in order to circumscribe the dimension to which they are committed: the redemption of pleasure, the halt of time, the absorption of death; silence, sleep, night, paradise – the Nirvana principle not as death but as life.
>
> (Marcuse 1955: 149)

Marcuse was interested in bringing to the fore positive models for the development of people and society. In contrast to many other psychoanalysts who saw mature genital-orientation and the solution of the Oedipus complex as normative preconditions for positive development, Marcuse claimed that such a development should absolutely not occur at the cost of the suppression of other types of libidinous impulses. The limited rationality represented by the father should not be allowed to suppress another type of libidinous rationality that is tied to the mother's proto-figure. According to Marcuse, society can change towards a Utopia and life instincts can overcome death instincts *only* through the promotion of a more all-embracing sexuality, including all forms of non-repressive sexuality.

Even though Marcuse's analyses can seem exaggerated and rather too Utopian, in many ways he anticipated a discussion that is still relevant. He also showed us how psychoanalytical theory can be used in a flexible way to frame questions about the various versions of social reality.

The social psychologist on the couch

I have chosen to discuss three theoreticians who were inspired by psycho-analytic theory. They are, of course, only a small selection from the count-less theoreticians and analyses that have been inspired by Freud and psychoanalysis in one way or another. When discussing the relation between psychoanalysis and social psychology, it is hard to avoid the question of how fruitful it is to base studies of societal change on a theory that is focused on the internal, psychological world of the individual. Do social psychologists have a place on the couch or should they instead focus on social interaction without worrying about what is happening in the minds of those doing the interacting?

In terms of determining how people in Western society form their thoughts about the body, sexuality, psychological development and person-ality types, psychoanalysis has been paradigmatic. Although many people are critical of what is now a very comprehensive and multifaceted theore-tical perspective, one can hardly avoid being confronted with it. Psycho-analysis is a natural point of departure for those who do not want to just observe human behaviour, but who also want to look at other aspects such as feelings, thoughts, ideas and bodily sensations. The respect for human integrity and for the specific logic of the inner life that characterizes psycho-analysis constitutes a counterweight to those theories in which humans are considered to be rational beings, whose image of themselves and the world around them is always fairly 'realistic'.

However, using psychoanalytical theory in a social psychological analy-sis is a difficult undertaking. In order to contribute to an analysis of society, the concepts and ideas of psychoanalysis must maintain their sharpness. Thus, we must consider how we can apply various notions to a social psychological theory. When psychoanalytical concepts are used too crudely in the social sciences, they commonly lose a great deal of their original meaning. In some cases, such analyses tend to take on an absurd character. Society is quite simply transformed into a patient who is placed on the couch and analysed. How can this be avoided?

We distinguish between a direct and an indirect application of psycho-analytic theory. Instead of taking the direct approach, it is sometimes sen-sible to either allow psychoanalytic theory to colour the analysis of society and contribute to a certain focus, or to reformulate the concepts, thereby building a bridge from the individual to the societal level of analysis. Elias' theory is a good example of just such an application of psychoanalysis.

When framing questions about the individual and society, the use of psychoanalysis can be advantageous.

It is also important to maintain some type of distinction between the logic that marks the inner world and the logic that guides people's everyday behaviour. Psychoanalysis is a conflict theory in which the non-verbal is pitted against the verbal, the pre-Oedipal against the Oedipal, and instincts and fantasy against culture. Even if we must now begin to modify the theory and think about how we should approach its dualistic notions, there is still no easy way to get around them. This problem is illustrated by the distinction between the real and the symbolic father. Even if the point of departure of our theorizing is a concrete social reality, for example, the nuclear family, people's interpretations and experiences of this 'reality' are seldom identical. Thus, the relation between social reality and the inner psychological world of symbols is extremely elastic and changeable.

Psychoanalysis has contributed to the elucidation and systematic study of the dark and forbidden sides of the psyche and human behaviour. It would not be a science if it merely made everything self-evident. Psychoanalysis helps us to bring to the fore questions that would otherwise be passed over, and to develop a language for experiences on the edge as well as for subtle emotional events. By inspiring thoughts about how emotional forces affect visible behaviour, the theory helps us to focus and frame questions about contradictions, ambivalences, destructive forces and other threats to the social order. Thus, in this way, psychoanalysis serves as a guarantor against the trivialization of social science and social psychology.

In this chapter, I have touched on some of the ideas generated within the context of psychoanalytical theorizing. I have chosen three theoreticians on the basis of their different approaches to modernity. Walter Benjamin helps us in our thinking about the impact of mass media, changing perceptions and the city as a mental environment. I will return to Benjamin's thoughts in the chapter on media culture. Norbert Elias opens a space for theorizing about the disciplined and controlled body. His thoughts on discipline, restraint and character formation will be followed up in the thematic chapter on the social psychology of the body. And finally, we have Herbert Marcuse, who has inspired me in my thinking about issues of sexuality, gender identities and repression. Even though I do not constantly refer to Marcuse, he has inspired much of the reasoning presented in the chapters on narcissism and gender identity.

Notes

1 Translation K.W.
2 Translation K.W.

3 The philosophy of the present and the dilemma of sociability

With the eyes of the Other

The expression 'symbolic interactionism' came from Herbert Blumer (Blumer 1937). However, before this term was coined in 1937, a large part of the philosophically and pragmatically oriented perspective with which it dealt had already been developed in Chicago by people such as Mead, Znaniecki and Park. It is difficult to describe this tradition in terms of an integrated theoretical perspective. Instead, it represents a specific way of approaching questions of identity, change and social interaction. It is not my intention to elucidate the differences between various interactionists or to report on the most important milestones in the area of interactionism.[1] Instead, I would like to illustrate the possibilities and limitations encompassed within this perspective, especially as they concern the social psychological study of the age in which we live.

At the beginning of the last century, the type of interactionism that was articulated in various contexts in Chicago was marked by a strong focus on pragmatics. That is, the purpose of interactionism was to understand social life and its changes by looking at people's actions. The focus of the analyses was on the active creation of sociability. It was interesting – in this constantly changing environment – to study how people approached themselves and the world around them. The social behaviourism that was developed by George Herbert Mead was characterized by a great confidence in people's resources and in their ability to change the present. The 'person' we meet in Mead's notes and papers is largely disengaged from traditions, religious ideas and biology. The individual is plastic – always prepared to change his or her own life and other people's lives. The self and social life are constantly in motion, and society is created through actions that always take place in the present. Social life is objectivized through people's actions. Mead says:

> In so far as the world is passing into a future, there is an opportunity for that which is not objective to become objective.
>
> (Mead 1938: 613)

Also emphasized in the interactionist tradition is the significance of action and the constant settling up with the past. In contrast to psychoanalysis, in which the problem to be understood is how the past is manifested in the present, the focus of interactionism is on how the present influences the past – on how humans constantly reconstruct their histories, creating new stories about themselves and other significant individuals. Thus, the central units of analysis are the social situation and its definition: the meeting between people and human action. In *The Philosophy of the Present*, Mead writes:

> In this attitude we are relating in our anticipation presents that slip into others, and their pasts belong to them. They have to be reconstructed as they are taken up into a new present and as such they belong to that present, and no longer to the present out of which we have passed into the present present.
>
> (Mead [1932] 1959: 22)

The self is always treated as an object that is scrutinized, reflected on and changed. People's ability to 'see themselves through the eyes of others' is the most important prerequisite for the creation of identity. This process, however, never stops at the mirroring itself, but is always tied to a reflexive component – the person's own standpoint on what Mead calls the *Generalized Other*. This reflexive component is composed of countless internalizations of societal norms, values and rules, all of which constitute a precondition for the individual's social existence.

Mead's individual – like Simmel's *stranger* and Park's *Marginal Man* – is in many ways indeterminable. And if there is something of substance in the recurring descriptions of the self and identity within interactionism, it is just this *paradigm of changeability*. People are not simply who they are, but instead who they become. Thus, we are dealing with a featureless individual who has great potential for change and for an active construction of the self. Memories are reconstrued in the light of the challenges met by the individual in the present. In other words, the past exists only as a social construction.

One theme adopted by Mead, and many interactionists that followed him, dealt with the reflexive process that allows the individual to gradually free himself or herself from traditions and the limitations set by biology. In interactionistic theorizing, this focus on the changeable individual sometimes leads to neglect of the surrounding world – social life and the culture.

However, the most interesting interactionistic studies often include discussions of cultural and sociomaterial change.

Within interactionism, many of the discoveries that were made at the beginning and middle of this century are now staple commodities of our sociological thinking. Today, the emphasis on social interaction, the self as a process, reflexivity, the constant reconstruction of life histories, subjectivization-objectivization, action and so on, constitute important elements of every social psychological analysis.

The advantage of the interactionistic view is that its theoretical core and understanding of the self are so intimately interwoven with modernity. Thus, this view will probably constitute a part of the social psychological understanding of social life long into the future, although it will certainly take different forms. If we want to follow the path of interactionism up until contemporary analysis, it is impossible to avoid Erving Goffman. This creative social psychologist represents a bridge between the type of interactionism that was developed in Chicago at the beginning of the 1900s and the analyses of late modernity that have been developed during the early 1990s by authors such as Giddens, Bauman and Beck.[2]

Erving Goffman at the crossroads of 'late modernity'

Even though Goffman's explicit ambitions were not to characterize cultural changes, he succeeded in conveying something essential about contemporary life through his microanalyses of social interaction. The reason Goffman is still popular and applicable today is that he developed concepts and analyses that pointed out central aspects of the logic of late-modern society. Although Goffman worked within the framework of a rather narrow interactionistic view, he also stepped outside of this perspective. In this way, he was able to make important observations about the times in which he lived and to give us insight into the contributions an interactionistic analysis of emotions and social characters can make in studies of the culture. If we follow Goffman's academic development, we can roughly distinguish three contemporary diagnostic areas of focus. The observations made by Goffman in his papers on the presentation of the self, psychiatric care and the ritualization of everyday life are still relevant to an understanding of late modernity.

In 1956, when Goffman published *The Presentation of Self in Everyday Life* and introduced the notion that society can be analysed using a theatre metaphor, he simultaneously provided the social sciences with a number of now well-known concepts (Goffman [1956] 1994). These concepts – among them personal façade, tact, front and back regions and mask – have proved to be useful in analyses of the media-saturated society, the youth culture and the aesthetization of everyday life. The publication of Goffman's book was timely. The American youth culture – with its music and expression of style

– was becoming the model for a global, Western youth culture, and the increased importance of the media in society was creating a greater awareness of the significance of wearing the right clothes, using the right language and being modern. The concept of *mask* captures the existential problem of the search for an authentic identity – a search that began with the members of the avant-garde, but that now constitutes a central element of most people's identity project.

At the beginning of the 1960s – when Goffman wrote his classic book about the asylum and described the forces of dehumanization at work behind the mental hospital's closed doors – he was one of the first to criticize the outlook on humankind that dominated mental health care. His criticism took hold in the growing antipsychiatry movement in England, among other places, and also in the general criticism of the hegemony of the medical model. The analyses formulated by Goffman in *Asylums* and *Stigma* are still relevant points of departure for a criticism of the medicalization and objectivization of humankind that marks today's psychiatric care (Goffman [1963] 1972, [1961] 1991).

During the 1960s and 1970s, Goffman developed various thoughts and ideas from his earlier studies of human interaction. What comes to the fore in Goffman's subtle analyses of interaction rituals, emotional strategies and protection mechanisms is a theory of the problem of narcissism for contemporary man. Again, Goffman was one of the first to examine the subtle mechanisms that characterize the social interactions of modern people. Although he does not pay great attention to cultural factors or to descriptions of the social milieu, a complex of problems of identity is presented that can be understood only in relation to the drastic changes taking place in the culture: the growth of a culture of consumption, the increased influence of the media in society and the explosion of styles and modes of expression in the big cities. Without doing too much violence to Goffman's analyses, we can incorporate them into a discourse on modernity, the goal of which is to place social interaction in a larger cultural context.

At this point, I will discuss in more detail Goffman's contribution to symbolic interactionism and, also, how we may be able to integrate his contribution into a discussion of late modernity.

The theatre metaphor

The analysis of society presented in *The Presentation of Self in Everyday Life* is based largely on the use of the theatre metaphor. Thus, social reality is analysed using concepts from the world of theatre. The dramaturgical analysis method, however, was heavily criticized and even Goffman himself eventually turned away from this type of analysis of social reality. But in spite of the criticism, certain dramaturgical concepts have survived. And the question is whether or not Goffman's analyses work irrespective of their connection to theatre concepts.

A good point of departure for a discussion of Goffman's dramaturgical efforts is his own example from a study of a local community on the Shetland Islands:

> For the last four or five years the island's tourist hotel has been owned and operated by a married couple of crofter origins. From the beginning, the owners were forced to set aside their own conceptions as to how life ought to be led, displaying in the hotel the full array of middle-class services and amenities. Lately, however, it appears that the managers have become less cynical about the performance that they stage; they themselves are becoming middle class and more enamored of the selves that their clients impute to them.
>
> (Goffman [1956] 1994: 24)

Cynical behaviour – based on the individual's constant development of a certain distance from how he or she performs and experiences himself or herself at work, in the family and in, for example, clubs and associations – is a precondition for the creation of self-understanding. But sometimes we lose our distance from a role and are swept up in it. Consider, for example, workaholics who no longer have a work self and a private self, but who *are* their work. According to Goffman's perspective, trying out these roles and masks is not without risk. It is, of course, possible to develop a distance from the role and to choose whether the mask should be put on or taken off. But the playing of the game itself is also a part of identity formation. The workaholic has become stuck in his or her role and the mask has hardened. This cynical role-taking can grow into a suit of armour and an inability to think reflexively. Thus, social life has more decisive consequences for people's identities than the theatre life has for its actors.

Goffman's reasoning on roles does not have the character of a static theory about how we take on and abandon various roles. Instead, he uses the concept of roles in order to analyse the perilous game that modern men and women play with different identities. We can take only a partial distance from social life. The more or less clear rules that guide our interplay with other people have a compelling force. But we can also experiment with these rules; we can consciously use social rules in order to present ourselves in such a way that those around us accept our claimed identity. When Goffman talks about 'impression management' he is referring to subtle mechanisms such as these.

Through the growth of the media and the image culture that has developed in late-modern society, people's awareness of the importance of a conspicuous identity has increased. The growth of occupational groups and social strata that deal exclusively with style production and aesthetics has contributed to the fact that, today, many people have developed an extremely refined ability to manage the impressions they make. This type of self-awareness also demands a high degree of reflexivity and self-discipline. Goffman shows how the identity and the body are successively drawn into the whirlpool of modernity.

Another of Goffman's concepts is the distinction between the front and back regions. The basic idea behind this distinction is that the individual exerts a high degree of self-control in the front regions, whereas, in the back regions, he or she dares to relax and let down his or her mask. But even if the stage concept is a natural starting point for such a discussion, this analysis has wider implications, in that it deals with contemporary humans' constant fluctuations between control and full expression. The mental image used by Goffman has been given a broader meaning in the contemporary culture.

This interplay between a disciplined approach and one in which experiences are recognized need not necessarily be associated with different spatially defined regions, but instead constitutes a dynamic that marks modern people's approach to themselves. Goffman also suggests that the relation between front and back regions can be expressed in many different ways. The emotionology of late modernity is characterized by people who are more and more skilled at presenting themselves and at choosing the right time to 'let go' of their self-control. Of course, this interplay is still associated with specific locations and regions, but the meaning of these physical spaces is always being reconstructed.

In a society marked by great detraditionalization, it is increasingly difficult for people to attach their identities to the obvious. Thus, in this way, every day is an adventure. The identity is constantly reconstructed in social interactions with others. However, an identity process that is so strongly situationally conditioned also leads to a state in which people become more dependent on one another and on how their own claimed identities are received by others. Concepts such as tact, dramaturgical loyalty, discipline, encounters and face engagement are useful in analyses of how individuals deal with the contingencies that often characterize life in late modernity. As long as people follow 'the rules of the game', the interplay with other individuals works. But when critical situations arise – situations in which the individual's presentation of the self is questioned – the instability and fragility of social life become quite clear. Along with the increased questioning and loss of legitimacy of traditions, norms and values follows more demands on the individual to develop an ability to communicate his or her experiences, feelings and opinions, and to clearly formulate his or her claimed identity.

There is no doubt that the theatre metaphor has certain analytical limitations. Concepts such as role manuscript, scene, back and front regions and dramaturgical loyalty need to be freed from the language of the theatre, but the ideas that Goffman elaborates in *The Presentation of Self in Everyday Life* are worth developing. In my opinion, many of the metaphors that

Goffman uses in his successful book are redundant and can be replaced by social psychological concepts. Today, instead of using the role concept, we talk about identity, and concepts such as dramaturgical loyalty have been replaced by phenomenological concepts such as trust and ontological security. But the main focus remains. Goffman also continued to develop his analyses of everyday life and critical environments. This is especially clear in his books about stigmatization and total institutions.

Identity, stigmatization and resistance

At the beginning of the 1960s, Goffman wrote two books in which he dealt with stigmatization and society's attempts to define and exclude certain people. In *Asylums* we find the most powerful analysis of this. Here, he describes not only what happens when a person resides in a total institution (prisons, mental hospitals and so on), but also how this person tries desperately to maintain some form of a sphere of intimacy and self-esteem.

Goffman begins the book with a thorough analysis of what he calls *the process of mortification*. From the first day the individual is registered at, for example, a mental hospital and becomes a patient, the process of de-humanization has begun. The individual's clothes and many of his human rights are taken from him, he is treated and defined as an object, and he is judged primarily in terms of his status as a psychiatric patient. Rather than curing those individuals who are subject to this type of care system, these total institutions participate in robbing them of their rights and human qualities. Goffman, however, not only presents a fateful account of how people are broken down and stripped of their humanity, he also shows us the potential they have for resistance and how they struggle to preserve their dignity.

The meagre existence in a total institution can be changed to a tolerable one if every opportunity for material and other types of improvement is taken. Among other things, Goffman talks about *make-dos* and *working the system*. The former concept refers to the creative use of all material objects that can be found at the institution. Spoons are transformed into knives, and towels are used as pillows and backrests, and so on. But, in order to take advantage of the system, one must understand how it works. Some inmates become very skilled at extracting all possible advantages out of the system, that is, at *working the system*. Goffman describes just such a person:

> For example, one inmate, with prior experience in Lexington, on his first morning in the hospital had rolled himself a supply of roll-your-owns, obtained polish and done two pairs of his shoes, uncovered which fellow inmate had a large cache of detective stories, organized himself a supply of coffee by means of instant coffee and the hot-water

tap, and found himself a place in the group psychotherapy sessions, sitting up close and waiting quietly for a few minutes before beginning to build up what was to be an active role.

(Goffman [1961] 1991: 193)

The trick, however, is not only to take advantage of the system, but also to avoid the oppression and the power that is wielded within the framework of the system. By creating free zones and retreating to places that are not controlled by the personnel, patients can pursue 'forbidden' activities and cultivate some form of personality. The creation of private places where the personality can be developed and protected from the institution's dehumanizing effects is an important part of the patients' and inmates' resistance work. Such resistance can consist of both an avoidance of power and an active struggle against it. Avoidance of power is often accomplished by establishing free zones and private spaces, whereas more active, subversive activities can take various forms.

Thus, while hospitalization has clear negative consequences for individuals, they can also use their 'illness' to obtain advantages. By consciously playing up certain symptoms, a patient may be able to get a private room or other material advantages. There are also more active forms of subversive activity. Some patients steal food and/or other items, only to sell them again on the total institution's black market. In prisons, inmates bribe the guards and establish their own rules – rules that govern certain aspects of everyday prison life, and so on.

In order to preserve their humanity in these often destructive institutional environments, people must develop survival strategies. At times this is a question of creating and retreating to a private inner world, as does Goffman's bridge player:

> One depressed, suicidal alcoholic, apparently a good bridge player, disdained bridge with almost all other patient players, carrying around his own pocket bridge player and writing occasionally for a new set of competition hands. Given a supply of his favourite gumdrops and his pocket radio, he could pull himself out of the hospital world at will, surrounding all his senses with pleasantness.
>
> (Goffman [1961] 1991: 273)

Goffman's subtle analyses of total institutions not only help us to understand how a psychiatric hospital or a prison functions, but they are also useful when studying other similar milieux and situations. By focusing on the social psychology of resistance, Goffman shows how people in the most vulnerable situations are somehow able to work through and face the symbolic or physical violence to which they are exposed. Although the people portrayed in *Asylums* do not consciously work to overthrow institutional care and the total institution, they are at least able to retain something of their human dignity. The strategies developed in these repressive environments are a sign of people's ability to actively participate in the creation of social reality, even if this participation is at times quite minimalistic in nature.

Interaction, rituals and feelings

A number of Goffman's early articles, including analyses of the ritualization of everyday life, are collected in the volume *Interaction Ritual: Essays on Face-to-face Behaviour* (1972), first published in 1967. Although these articles were written while Goffman was also working on the formulation of his dramaturgical model, they do not contain any theatre metaphors. But the subtle analyses found in these articles on the mechanisms of everyday life are the same as those found in *The Presentation of Self in Everyday Life*, and it is easy to see how he would later couple them to the language of dramaturgy.

The point of departure of all of these articles is the notion that the individual's character is created in social interplay, and that this process is extremely delicate. When people put themselves on display, there is always a risk that they will lose face. In one exciting essay, Goffman analyses what happens when people fail to show the 'right face'. When we put ourselves and our faces on display, we are also exposing ourselves to public scrutiny. If a given presentation of a face fails and is called into question by others, the result can be a breakdown in the social interplay and the development of a feeling of disgrace.

In Goffman's analyses, various expressions of emotion indicate problems with self-presentation. For example, disgrace indicates that the individual has failed to win other people over to his or her side. At this point, he or she must try to re-establish his or her honour and dignity. When individuals' status and social position are threatened, they must often do emotional work in order to reduce the awkward aspects of their loss of honour and to, in the best case, re-establish their honour. Goffman describes this process in a footnote:

> At such moments 'joshing' sometimes occurs. It is said to be a means of releasing the tension caused either by embarrassment or by whatever caused embarrassment. But in many cases this kind of banter is a way of saying that what occurs now is not serious or real. The exaggeration, the mock insult, the mock claims – all these reduce the seriousness of conflict by denying reality to the situation. And this, of course, in another way, is what embarrassment does. It is natural, then, to find embarrassment and joking together, for both help in denying the same reality.
>
> (Goffman 1967: 112)

The ritualization of everyday life is an important aspect of the construction of society as a fairly coherent whole. Consisting of actions, symbols and gestures, this ritualization contributes – through social interaction – to the creation of the fairly stable structures we call a society. However, such a construction is fragile in nature. And it is just this fragility to which Goffman constantly returns. People are always busy trying to uphold certain social patterns, but they often fail.

If we want our social life to function, the basic rule is to avoid all situations that can threaten the provisional equilibrium that has been established. Goffman writes:

> Social life is an uncluttered, orderly thing because the person voluntarily stays away from the places and topics and times where he is not wanted and where he might be disparaged from going. He cooperates to save his face, finding that there is much to be gained from venturing nothing.
>
> (Goffman 1967: 43)

The philosophy of avoidance is a prerequisite for the painless functioning of social life. This often occurs according to routine, with the individual reflecting neither on why he or she acted in a specific way nor on why he or she avoids certain places and situations.

The view developed by Goffman in *Interaction Ritual* is based on the temporary nature of life and on humankind's attempts to deal with the contingencies generated in modernity by ritualizing everyday life and developing a specific emotionology. This ritualization can be thought of as an attempt to create some kind of permanence in life. Goffman inexorably reveals the chimera-like character of life and the individual's fatal attempts to establish an identity. Only when the individual dares to expose himself or herself to criticism and to be called in question can his or her character be changed. Goffman writes: 'The self, in brief, can be voluntarily subjected to re-creation'. To act *actively* is the same as risking something. Heroic individuals are not content with maintaining the society as it is, they also want to change and to influence social development. In studying Goffman's analyses of all the subtle processes that guide our actions and that cause us to put self-esteem before self-development, it is clear that displaying such heroics is no simple task.

By experimenting with a few imaginative concepts, Goffman succeeds in describing the structuring process that leads to the reproduction of what we call society. The strength of his analysis is that he shows us how fragile the structures we call society actually are. He demonstrates that the basis for the existence of these structures is the fact that people follow the implicit and explicit rules that govern social interactions. Additionally, he shows how hard it is to break these rules. Much of the emotionology sketched out by Goffman deals with how people protect themselves from threats directed towards the individual's self-presentation and private life. For Goffman, the rituals of everyday life and protection mechanisms have a 'holy' character; that is, what seem to be trivial situations can have a great importance for how society works or does not work.

Even simple situations, such as when we make eye contact with another person, can reveal a great deal about how we function in society. What Goffman calls 'civil inattention' is one of the fundamental tenets of the rule book of social interaction (Goffman 1967). He is referring here to the ability to determine how long we are allowed to look at another person. Because this time period is often carefully regulated, it is tempting to break this rule. Using sunglasses, hidden glances, mirrors and other aides, people are able to get a glimpse of that which is forbidden. For example, studying the body of a person of the opposite sex at the gym is considered to be impolite. But by using the numerous mirrors installed in such places and a subtle voyeuristic technique, people are able to examine each other's half-naked bodies. Staring at another person for too long is considered to be almost a sick behaviour. According to Goffman, an individual's inadequate knowledge of the rules that govern social interaction can even contribute to his or her being defined as deviant.

Goffman helps us to direct our attention to the seemingly trivial situations of everyday life and to, thereby, discover numerous interesting details. These situations play a direct and decisive role in how society is structured. We also gain insight into the complex emotionology that guides our actions and that is an important part of the structuring process. Although Goffman does not tie his in-depth studies of social interaction to arguments about the big city, the media-saturated society and other more general structuring processes, these social and cultural transformations are still present by virtue of their absence, but one has to, so to speak, read between the lines. Goffman's concepts are neither centred on the individual nor intended only to describe social interaction; thus, they help us to develop a theoretical bridge between individual and society.

The philosophy of the moment and the compulsion of the situation

Symbolic interactionism puts into focus that which is happening in the present. This is both its strength and its weakness. It creates the necessary preconditions for studying everyday life as something more general than trivial encounters between people. Many of the concepts developed within the framework of this tradition are now staple commodities in the social sciences. As mentioned earlier, symbolic interaction is the child of modernity. The questions that were formulated were typical of the times, but are still relevant today. Individualism, which is also a strong ideological force within interactionism, has contributed to the situation today in which many people assume that they can affect their own life and the lives of others. This assumption – that it is possible to create oneself, to sculpt the body and to develop a positive identity – is based on the notion that social life is largely constructed. Accordingly, our momentary actions are meaningful and lead us somewhere.

It was Goffman who developed some of the basic assumptions of inter-actionism. By studying theoreticians who were interested in cultural change and structures, such as Simmel, Elias and Lévi-Strauss, Goffman was able to develop concepts that are still useful in our studies of contemporary life. In contrast to those theoreticians who focused exclusively on the conse-quences of individualization for the individual and society, Goffman shows how the loosening of traditions and structures results in the creation of new oases of security. The ritualization of everyday life is central to the under-standing of contemporary culture. The process implies two things: first, that new opportunities for mutual consensus are constantly created; and, second, that an emotionology is developed that allows people to develop a subtle ability to control their emotional lives and to exert the degree of self-control necessary in different situations.

In his studies, Goffman portrays an individual without features. This person lacks a cultural and social background and has no explicit ideas about the future. He exists exclusively in the present. He is occupied with develop-ing strategies that will allow him to deal with the compulsion of the situation. This individual has a great capacity to break the rules and to overstep various boundaries. The creativity and inventiveness shown by the inmates of total institutions, the clever strategies used for stepping outside the role manu-script, and the ritualized life all bear witness to the marked human capacity to reflect and to absorb knowledge about the workings of the system.

It was certainly not Goffman's ambition to devise a theory of how we are affected by the past or of how Utopias and desires can lead us into the future. But it is on just these points he came up short. When we have analysed a social situation and understand the forces that affect people's actions within a given framework, our interest in the wider context that led to the specific situation and to just these patterns of behaviour and rituals is awakened. And we also begin to wonder where the processes we have studied will lead. Will the relationship we have studied, for example, between men and women at their place of work, be changed in the future? What might con-tribute to such a change? On these points, Goffman fails to give us the answers, and we must therefore turn to other theoreticians in order to dis-cover the mechanisms that either lead to the status quo or to actual change.

Notes

1 For a detailed discussion of the development of interactionism, see, for example, Meltzer *et al.* (1975) and Denzin (1992).
2 In the following presentation, I have clearly taken my inspiration from Giddens' interpretation of Goffman's authorship (Giddens 1984).

4 Reflexive modernity and social psychology

Everyday life and social psychology towards the millennium

During the 1980s and 1990s, words such as *modernity* and *postmodernity* have occurred frequently in the social science literature. However, the meaning attached to these concepts has shifted. This variation at times reflects disagreement about how the concepts should be defined, but it is also a consequence of the different ways in which contemporary Western society can be looked at and analysed. But if we consider modernists' and postmodernists' radically different opinions about various societal phenomena, we find that these differences are often constructed and unnecessarily polarized in nature. Although they use different terms to describe our age, they often study similar processes of change. But, of course, their interpretations of these processes vary. These differences in opinion and interpretation often result in competitive attempts to arrive at the absolute truth about society. But such differences should be viewed positively and encouraged, as they allow us to reveal more aspects of the phenomenon under study.

Discussions about modernity/postmodernity often presuppose a static view of so-called *traditional societies*. This polarized way of looking at the relation between the traditional and the modern is deeply rooted in the social sciences.[1] However, during recent years, such an absolute distinction between the old and the new has been questioned. Some researchers claim that traditional societies are more differentiated and modulated than sociologists and other social scientists have thought, and that contemporary Western society still has deep and solid roots in history and traditions. In discussions of contemporary life, there is a clear tendency for researchers to focus solely on change and to exaggerate its importance. Without delving too deeply into this complicated topic, we can state that a degree of caution should be used when attempting to contrast the old and the new. This is, of course, also the case when making historical comparisons of various points in time during the 1900s.

Even if it is not necessary to construct absolute dividing lines between the traditional and the modern, we can establish the fact that there are crucial differences between the traditional agrarian society and the industrial, information technology society of today. The processes of societal change described by the classic sociologists – urbanization, secularization and industrialization – and the contemporary processes of change referred to as globalization, mediazation and computerization, have all influenced and led to drastic changes in people's approach to their own life projects and to the world around them.

From a social psychological perspective, we are not primarily interested in overall societal and cultural changes, nor are we especially interested in the internal psychological processes that are a consequence of these transformations. Instead, we want to understand how people choose to structure and approach their day-to-day lives and their life projects. Our focus, thus, is on living in and experiencing modernity (Berman 1987, Bauman 1990, Featherstone 1991b). But, in order to gain knowledge about this intermediary level of analysis, we must take an interest in both the overall changes taking place in our time and in people's inner reactions to these changes.

The experience of living in modernity is often described as a combination of a longing for cultural roots and an insight into the fact that everything is changeable and transient. It is precisely this enormous chasm between stability, security and unchangeability, on the one hand, and insecurity, changeability and dissolution, on the other, that characterizes the experience of modernity. Paul Auster has captured this experience in his essay *The Locked Room*, which begins as follows:

> It seems to me now that Fanshawe was always there. He is the place where everything begins for me, and without him I would hardly know who I am. We met before we could talk, babies crawling through the grass in diapers, and by the time we were seven we had pricked our fingers with pins and made ourselves blood brothers for life. Whenever I think of my childhood now, I see Fanshawe. He was the one who was with me, the one who shared my thoughts, the one I saw whenever I looked up from myself. But that was a long time ago. We grew up, went off to different places, drifted apart. None of that is very strange, I think. Our lives carry us along in ways we cannot control, and almost nothing stays with us. It dies when we do, and death is something that happens to us every day.
>
> (Auster 1985: 235)

What Auster describes is in many ways a common human experience that most of us recognize. We lose contact with our childhood friends and they all follow their own separate paths. Auster also emphasizes some of the features of late modernity: lack of control and predictability, constant separations from friends and relations, and the constant presence of death in the here and now.

The question is whether the ability to mourn might be one of the most important characteristics of contemporary man. In society today, we are constantly forced to separate from people, and we are also aware of the fact that many relationships are temporary, that there is always the chance that friends will leave, move to another country, develop in another direction and so on. The emotionology of breaking away and saying goodbye is of central importance to our understanding of the situation of contemporary man. In order to separate from close friends and relatives, the individual must develop the ability to deal with loss and grief.

In his article from 1917, *Mourning and Melancholia*, Freud discusses what happens when we are unable to confront the sorrow and loss associated with a separation (Freud [1917] 1984). The individual either develops melancholy as a sign of his or her inability to separate from the actual person and from the internal representation of the person, or he or she becomes manic, desiring to replace this loss with a new object and thereby denying the loss. In order to handle the grief and go on with life, individuals must learn to deal with ambivalence. They must learn to combine both the love and hate they feel towards the person who has abandoned them, and then to work through the loss without denying it.

Is there a difference between the type of social psychology that Simmel formulated at the beginning of the twentieth century and the discussion of reflexive modernization that I am introducing here by taking up the social psychology of grief? Isn't this the same homelessness, individualization, identity crisis and so on that has been focused on ever since Simmel's time? The answer is both yes and no. In a way, we are still discussing the same historical process of change, but we are able to observe an intensification of the process. If agreeing with Simmel, we might say that the same social forms are being analysed, but that they have been filled with a radically new content.

The type of social psychology that was formulated within the framework of a paradigm of modernity is clearly a Western construct. The analyses have mainly centred on the consequences of the process of individualization for identity formation. There has sometimes been a tendency to forget to connect these processes to questions about societal and social problems; such connections were a central part of the efforts made in, for example, the Chicago school. In the world today, it is increasingly important to discuss how the breakdown of old structures and traditions affects people's everyday lives and identities. It is also important to study the different consequences general social and cultural changes have for people from different social strata – men as compared with women and among individuals with different ethnic backgrounds.

In order to make the consequences of individualization fully understandable, we must study how this cultural process of change intervenes in specific social contexts. Today, it is not enough to focus solely on class or gender, for example, but we must address the complexity that is created in the interaction between various sociocultural factors. On the whole, it is necessary to try to discuss the consequences of modernity in as detailed a way as possible, and to embrace both a sceptical attitude towards the cult of individuality and an ability to emphasize changes – although these changes do not always have an unambiguous and unproblematic character and direction.

In order to arrive at a more modulated view of the overall cultural change that we find in discussions of modernity, I will focus on the emotionology and the various cognitive strategies that have been developed in order to deal with the consequences of the processes of detraditionalization and individualization. Today, in the context of the postmodernity debate, scientists have also become interested in the complex social psychology of emotions. If we are to have a chance of studying contemporary life from a social psychological perspective, we must be able to address the often paradoxical and contradictory social and cultural processes that are involved in the construction of the late-modern identity.

Late modernity and institutional reflexivity

Discussions about modernity include many different dimensions and aspects, but I have chosen to emphasize those that concern the development of institutional reflexivity. This phenomenon must be understood in relation to at least three additional structural factors: the process of individualization, detraditionalization and the emergence of risk environments.

Anthony Giddens defines institutional reflexivity as: 'The regularised use of knowledge about circumstances of social life as a constitutive element in its organisation and transformation' (Giddens 1991: 20). What we call reflexivity – that is, the ability to constantly scrutinize and evaluate one's own self-identity project – is not primarily a creation of the individual. This increased reflexivity is well rooted in the project of modernity. In a society where explanations such as 'that's how we've always done it' and 'that's how God has willed it' are seldom accepted – a society where the search for knowledge and the examination of established facts are an integral part of social life – people are sentenced to reflexivity. In order to discuss institutional reflexivity at all, we must first look more closely at two central historical processes.

The concept of *individualization* is often used rather carelessly to denote those changes that resulted in an increased focus on individuals and their ability to realize their life goals. This process, however, can just as easily lead to increased disciplinization and control of people as it does to increased freedom. The fact that people are released from historically based traditions and social ties does not mean that they are automatically able to choose how they want to live their lives. For better or worse, individualization has made the individual the centre of our attention.

Ulrich Beck differentiates between *full value individualization* and *the individualization of poverty* (Beck [1993] 1996). This distinction refers to people's varying life conditions and abilities to take advantage of the opportunities created by the breakdown of traditions and of the social collective. On the one hand, there are people who have the time, resources and abilities to engage themselves in the development of a specific lifestyle and to realize their dreams. On the other hand, however, there are people who lack such prerequisites and who are frustrated by the discrepancy between their unbounded dreams of happiness and their actual life circumstances. Today, it is difficult to avoid being affected by the consequences of individualization, but the effects vary as a function of the individual's social status and cultural affiliation.

Another aspect of individualization is the increased opportunity for social control that is a side-effect of this process. When individuals are distributed across more and more different lifestyles, social groups, subcultures, personality types, diagnostic categories and so on, it is easier to design everything, from advertisement and public profiles to an advanced system of government control. Individualization makes certain social groups and individuals more conspicuous. But this also means that there are other groups that are invisible. Thus, it is in this way that the process of individualization is always double-edged, implying greater freedom for certain individuals and groups and less freedom for others.

Detraditionalization implies that people are less and less able to take things for granted. Even deeply rooted rituals and cultural patterns – for example, the celebration of Christmas, marriage, the division of labour in the home – are drawn into a reflexive process, and this leads to the insight that there are many ways to celebrate Christmas and to divide household chores. This does not mean that traditions are discarded completely, but that their changeability and plasticity are discovered. Thus, the meaning of tradition is transformed and we can call into question the relevance of this concept in late-modern society. Today, traditions are even consciously constructed and used in order to defend certain ideals and to legitimate a certain activity. We can observe a strong tendency towards nostalgia and an adoration of everything, from old, 'honourable' values and rituals to an enthusiastic interest in old things that are highly valued as objects of consumption and fetishes.

As traditions lose their value as landmarks and security factors in life, individuals are increasingly left to themselves and to the know-how and facts they can accumulate and use as a basis for their decisions. In a society where our view of knowledge is always changing, everything from social institutions to everyday life must be permeated with a readiness to re-evaluate activities and actions. Thus, institutional reflexivity is an increasingly important component of all social behaviour. There is always a better way to bake a cake, do psychotherapy, build a house, play rock 'n' roll, run an organization, live your life and so on.

This increased focus on knowledge and on a scientific view of society and its individuals are both a part of modernity. For better and for worse. This process has a flipside. Beck has indicated how Western society is developing more and more towards what he calls a risk society (Beck [1986] 1992). Beck describes the mechanisms that lead to the development of such a society as follows:

> Risks such as those produced in the late modernity differ essentially from wealth. By risks I mean above all radioactivity, which completely evades human perceptive abilities, but also toxins and pollutants in the air, the water and foodstuffs, together with the accompanying short- and long-term effects on plants, animals and people. They induce systematic often *irreversible* harm, generally remain *invisible*, are based on causal interpretations, and thus initially only exist in terms of (scientific and anti-scientific) *knowledge* about them. They can thus be changed, magnified, dramatized or minimized within knowledge, and to that extent they are particularly *open to social definition and construction*. Hence the mass media and the scientific and legal professions in charge of defining risks become key social and political positions.
>
> (Beck [1986] 1992: 22ff, emphasis in original)

Institutional reflexivity has no aim. It presupposes that there is a director controlling the course of events, which without such control would easily get off track. Someone must decide how knowledge will be used and how the continuous process of change that is created through reflexivity will influence people's lives. When we begin to address questions such as these, we are forced to talk about power.

In a society that is based increasingly on the information industry, the empire of experts also expands. Institutional reflexivity is founded on an always growing number of experts, all with their own specialities. Although some of this knowledge can be used to create the conditions for a good life for the man on the street, there are even risks that this expert-made knowledge will be used to promote economic and political interests that are contrary to the needs and interests of the citizens. Thus, institutional reflexivity – the purpose of which is to support an ongoing discussion of how we can and should understand and explain social reality – opens the doors to a symbolic struggle over who has the right to define and set the agenda for how we approach, for example, a specific social problem.

Beck shows us how such battles over definitions can take on absurd proportions. For example, the established limits for controlling the dumping of toxic chemicals, atomic waste and other environmentally harmful products always constitute a compromise between economic, political and human interests. But who, then, is responsible for determining the effects of the total amount of waste products? The scientific system that is responsible for setting the limits for toxic waste dumping has absolutely no capacity to survey the situation. Who is responsible for the more general risk estimates? In Beck's risk society, institutional reflexivity is marked by short-term decisions and the lack of a comprehensive view. This society is transformed into an enormous laboratory, where scientific thresholds are established for how much of something people can be subjected to before they react.

In today's society, we have great opportunities to choose our lifestyle and to approach other people in a number of different ways. It is also possible to use existing knowledge in order to experiment with various approaches to social reality and to oneself. No one has a monopoly on the truth. This can result in what Hannah Arendt calls 'the tyranny of possibilities' (cited in Bauman 1997: 73). Thus, there is a dark side to modernity. Just as institutional reflexivity can lead to a better life for most people, it can also lead to a feeling of hopelessness and resignation. If there is no ultimate truth, what do we have to hold on to? In a society where people do not have common frames of reference, clear goals or basic values and where individuality is embraced, loneliness and alienation grow easily, as does the exclusion of those people who cannot handle the tyranny of possibilities.

Although people react differently to the historical changes comprised in the notion of modernity, there are also common points of reference. Just such a general reference could be the feeling of contingency that has been described by Richard Rorty and others.

Contingency

The word *contingency* is well suited to the job of capturing the contradictory and ambivalent character of modernity. According to *Webster's Encyclopedic Dictionary* (1989), the word can mean possibility, fortuitousness, uncertainty and accident. Thus, it encompasses both the unlimited possibilities that are thought to characterize the project of modernity and the project's darker sides. When we later describe the *structure of feelings* that mark late modernity, we will constantly return to the experience of contingency.

In his book *Irony, Contingency and Solidarity* (1989), Richard Rorty has discussed in detail the uncertainty that characterizes much of modern life. The stories we develop about ourselves and the attempts we make to represent and explain our material and social reality do not bring us any closer to the absolute truth. It is rather the case that the linguistic signs and symbols we use are exceedingly preliminary in nature. On this point, Rorty speaks of: 'Increasingly useful metaphors rather than of increasing understanding of how things really are'.

Of course, the general quality of experience Rorty describes is an extremely variable phenomenon. Even if most people are affected by what we have called contingency – in the form of a loss of meaning and control in life – they react in very different ways. In certain societal strata, people cultivate these experiences and even employ them directly in their occupation or in a creative capacity. Devoting oneself to the search, uncertainty, 'the approaching catastrophe', and so on, can become part of a lifestyle. But uncertainty and insecurity can also be a strain. Some people live from day to day, not knowing if they will be able to support themselves and their families – they live in the modern society's dark backyard. The threat of nuclear war and environmental catastrophes also leads to a feeling of contingency, not to enthusiastic experimentation with the possibilities of contingency, but in the worst case to a feeling of hopelessness.

A life and an identity arise and are created in contact with other people and at the gentle pace of everyday life. But the more people ask existential questions about *life's meaning* or *the meaning of life,* the more they realize that there are no absolute answers. When Freud wrote his book about the interpretation of dreams at the beginning of this century, he set the agenda for discussions on the mysteries of personal identity. Dreams can certainly be explained and understood, but only to a certain degree. We are then left to the individual imagination, which weaves a story about a specific life and its meaning. Inspired by Nabokov's book *Pale Fire*, Rorty describes people's life project as follows:

> Nabokov built his best book, *Pale Fire*, around the phrase 'Man's life as commentary to abstruse unfinished poem'. That phrase serves both as a summary of Freud's claim that every human life is the working out of a sophisticated idiosyncratic fantasy, and as a reminder that no such working out gets completed before death interrupts. It cannot get completed because there is nothing to complete, there is only a web of relations to be rewoven, a web which time lengthens every day.
>
> (Rorty 1989: 42ff)

In late modernity, the general feeling of contingency has been manifested in various ways. It is somehow present by virtue of its absence, and people try desperately to orient themselves in their existence. They develop different search strategies. Thomas Ziehe has described three such strategies: *subjectivization, ontologization* and *potentialization* (Ziehe 1989).

The experience of society as an increasingly cold, impersonal and abstract place is counteracted by subjectivization. This is perhaps most clear in youth culture, where expressive locution, styles and interests are mixed and developed in order to accentuate subjectivity and intimacy. Young people seek out different subcultures or lifestyles in order to be somebody and to be part of a community. According to some researchers, we are living today in an experiential society. Such a cultural movement is probably engineered in order to counteract tendencies towards meaninglessness and hopelessness – or in order to charge life with meaning and develop confidence in the possibilities of the individual.

The loss of meaning can even lead to attempts to re-establish a belief in something. Everything from new-age spiritualism and political extremism, on the one hand, to involvement in the environmental or peace movements, on the other, can function as a counterbalance to the breakdown of traditions and meaning discussed earlier. Truth can never be definite in nature, but it is possible to recreate much of the feeling of monopolizing the truth that, for example, characterized the arrogance of high modernity.

Potentialization implies an acceptance of late modernity. By devoting himself or herself to intensive experiences and by constantly being on the move, the individual can counteract the feelings of emptiness and melancholy that mark the loss of meaning. Living just for today and not caring about anything can, paradoxically enough, create a solid point of departure. Trendy if rather dangerous sports, body building, various types of risk taking and so on are part of a concept that accepts and cultivates the intensification of the nerves – something that Simmel saw as a modern psychological problem.

The search for an identity can have many manifestations. But even though it concerns placing the individual at the centre, we are still talking about a collective search. Even the most personal project is drawn into the creation of new collective forms. And the most subversive individual phenomenon can be a part of a new social movement.

Neo-tribes and bodily acts

In the past, classical social formations – based, for example, on class affiliation and gender – were the foundation for collective identities. Nowadays, however, they have lost their status as self-evident starting points for discussions of identity formation. But even if people's approach to these types of collective identities has changed, this does not automatically imply that collective identities have lost all their importance or that we can no longer discern them. Instead, there would seem to be a continuous re-evaluation of previous collective identities, at the same time as new forms of collective affiliation have grown. I will first briefly discuss these tendencies, and then resume the discussion of the different strategies that can be used to deal with the conditions of late modernity.

It has probably never been the case that class, gender and ethnicity have served as separate categories. It is more likely that one or more of these collective categories have been emphasized during different historical periods.

For example, the question of class has historically been more important than that of gender. But whereas certain people have claimed that class must always be considered to be a basic category if we are to understand oppression and exploitation, feminists have claimed that the oppression of women should be the most important question. In the labour movement, the weighing of such issues has been of central importance. The awareness that oppression is multifactorial has grown gradually. If we want to understand the formation of classical collective identities in today's society, we must study how, for example, class, gender and ethnicity combine to form complex patterns. A refugee woman who is unemployed might be found at one end of the continuum, and a white, well-educated, middle-class man with a high salary might be found at the other.

In a media-saturated society, it is possible to be part of collective formations that are not firmly localized in physical space. Affiliation with various lifestyles is determined by knowledge about, and visualizations of, a specific cultural affiliation. Although the group members do not actively interact with each other, a feeling of belonging can be created. Within idol cultures, people develop emotional ties to cult objects as well as to other individuals with the same interests. In this way, a feeling of belonging is created that is based on similar experiences and preferences. A similar type of collective identity can be felt among interrailers, bikers, hackers and members of other lifestyle groups. Such abstract identities have at times been called *neo-tribes* (Maffesoli 1996).

New types of collective identities can even be formed through the establishment of social groups that are committed to a specific social question – for example, the environment, peace, animal research or religion. In contrast to neo-tribes, these social groups are more tangible in nature; the members meet in order to discuss political or religious strategies and events. It is often the case that such critical communities are formed in opposition to another, already existing collective formation or group, or in order to promote a new way of understanding and addressing social and cultural questions.

The various collective identities and groups that develop in late-modern society constitute different ways of approaching the overall changes we have previously dealt with and the experience of contingency. The more the most important relationships in people's lives take on the form of what Giddens calls *pure relations* – relationships that are based solely on the interchange and confirmation people derive from these relations rather than on traditional ties or conventions – the stronger grows the desire for security and belonging. At the same time, this breakdown of the solid ties between people and of conventions can also aid those individuals who want to change our relationship patterns and create new types of social relations and identities.

We can roughly differentiate between two types of ontologization. On the one hand, we have various types of fundamentalism and identity politics, the purpose of which is to emphasize a certain outlook on life or a certain collective identity. On the other hand, we have a minimalistic ontologization that has to do with anchoring the identity to, for example, the body or a certain type of adventure sport. Whereas the first variant is often associated with different kinds of fanaticism and extremism, the other variant of ontologization constitutes a combination of the search for security, on the one hand, and a potentialization and subjectivization of life, on the other.

The collective identities that come to the fore in late-modern society can be characterized partly by extreme transiency, and partly by permanency and strong ties to old traditions. Many neo-tribes exist only for a short while and are replaced by other collective identities. But co-existing with these short-term and unstable collective formations, there is also the desire to re-establish traditions and to depict certain types of identities as more genuine and true than others. Such fundamentalism often occurs in religious contexts, but it is even quite prominent in contexts where the identities of marginalized and oppressed groups are emphasized. Even though the purpose of identity politics can be acceptable, such politics can easily turn into fundamentalism. An overly intense focus on one's own group affiliation and an unwillingness to be affected by people from other groups, often lead to rigid distinctions between in- and out-groups.

Today, in addition to these collective identity projects, we have many projects in which people pursue a minimalistic criticism of society. Through subversive bodily acts – in which the body is used to point out unnecessarily rigid distinctions between the sexes or to show how we can include the body in the formulation of a plastic and open identity – people can achieve the construction of an identity and go beyond existing approaches to the body. In a similar manner, involvement in personal political questions and sub-politics – politics that is initiated through the actions of citizens – can contribute to the development of new identities.

We can search for an identity through participation in collective movements, and even in our own bodies or through involvement in personal political questions. Many people vacillate between the desire to create a paradise where total security reigns and where they know exactly who they are and what they want in life, and the desire to embrace change and constant regeneration. But regardless of where on the continuum we do our identity formation, ontologization constitutes an important part of the late-modern individual's need to be anchored in his existence and to find solid points of departure in an otherwise chaotic social reality.

Self-reflexivity, style and irony

The development of the late-modern identity takes place through an ongoing reflexive process. The various goals, choices and actions formulated by the individual are scrutinized and revised continuously. This is done so that the life project the individual has worked out will hold water and form a fairly comprehensible *Gestalt*.

Because our age is marked by the production of an almost absurd amount of information and scientific know-how, it is difficult to avoid relating to different aspects of the reflexive self-identity project. Parents are updated on current discoveries in child development and rearing, young people are supplied with information on sex and, at work, the outlook on professionalism and the culture of organizations is always changing. Being kept this busy with one's personal identity can be experienced as positive and help people to grow, but it can also constitute a psychological strain. These continuous revisions of the identity and the experience of what seem to be unlimited possibilities to mould a more beautiful body, earn more money, and so on, result in an ongoing search for new successes and new experiences. And these successes must be visible if one's identity is to be affirmed.

In the late-modern culture, the heavy demands on self-presentation are most conspicuous in people's great awareness of the importance of style; a person's style clearly represents his or her public position and is a visualization of his or her success. Style functions both as a status marker and as an effective symbolization of what is new and of the desire for constant renewal. Thus, fashion has both a conservative character – in that it serves to maintain status differences and societal super- and subordination – and a function that is dynamic and allows us to diagnose our times. The diagnostic value of fashion lies in its ability to represent new tendencies in society.

But style involves much more than just fashion. Presenting oneself as positively as possible even requires the ability to use language and carry on a conversation in the 'right' way, to use the 'correct' body language and to design an overall aesthetically attractive lifestyle. Such an aesthetization of the individual requires considerable cultural competence, style consciousness and flexibility.

The reflexive self-identity project puts heavy demands on how individuals approach the world around them and themselves. In order to avoid this continuous examination of who we are and what we want out of life, some people develop an exceptionally sophisticated ability to use irony. But what is irony? *Collins English Dictionary* (1991: 816) defines it as follows:

> 1. The humorous or mildly sarcastic use of words to imply the opposite of what they normally mean. 2. An instance of this, used to draw attention to some incongruity or irrationality. 3. Incongruity between what is expected to be and what actually is, or a situation or result showing such incongruity.

The use of irony neutralizes the more serious self-examinations that mark late modernity. With irony, we can flip social reality upside down and avoid taking things seriously. Although the ironist makes fun of people who take the project of reflexivity seriously, they are also part of the same project.

In many ways, the reflexive individual and the ironist constitute two sides of the same coin. They can be viewed as two social types who reflect an essential contemporary complex of problems. The *reflexive* individual continuously examines themselves and their actions in relation to existing knowledge. They are used to dealing with the flow of information and to filtering out just the knowledge and information they need in order to complete a specific task. This person is characterized by a means-end rationality. In his description of the thoughtful personality, Freud comes close to the reflexive individual:

> In reflection there is one more physical activity at work than in the most attentive self-observation, and this is shown among other things by the tense looks and wrinkled forehead of a person pursuing his reflections compared with the restful expression of a self-observer.
>
> (Freud [1900] 1985: 175)

The *ironist*'s way of dealing with the flow of information is entirely different from that of the reflexive individual. Although the ironist is a skilled user of information and knowledge, their goal is not to be as clear as possible, but instead to cultivate vagueness. By juggling with linguistic meaning and using the diversity of language, the ironist is able to avoid being locked into categories. The ironist's behaviour can be interpreted as jocular and satirical commentary on the reflexivity project. Belief in the means-end rationality that marks this project is lacking. The ironist has no basic confidence in modernity. At the same time, in order to play their game, they skilfully use the symbols and information that are the products of contemporary society.

The ironist is the reflexive individual's alter ego. They make a sham of the reflexive individual's serious attempts to develop a story about themselves and their life. The ironist tries to show that it is impossible even to attempt to define people and arrange them in specific categories and identities. Thus, the ironist's efforts constitute a subtle criticism of contemporary rationality.

In contrast to the various emotional protection mechanisms that Simmel discussed, the creation of the social types described above is closely tied to the contemporary abstract culture. It is not a case of trying to escape all forms of cultural influence, but instead of allowing oneself to be drawn into the symbolic sphere and then using the cultural raw material in order to develop an identity. At times, the ironist and the reflexive individual are certainly both blasé and cynical. However, they do not show this by distancing themselves from the culture, but instead by participating in it even more actively. Thus, we are not dealing here with the emotionology of avoidance, but with the emotionology of ecstasy.

The emotionology of late modernity

In a society where traditions have lost their importance as creators of meaning and where it is difficult to claim that absolute knowledge about social reality exists, people must establish some form of ontological security. However, in contemporary society, such an ambition and need to develop a basic trust in people and social institutions must be elaborated in such a way that the diversity and insecurity that characterize this society are taken into account.

Late-modern humans constantly find themselves in situations where they must make a choice. And there is no way to know for certain how one should choose the right product, partner or profession. Choosing one thing even means distancing oneself from another. People attempt to reduce the number of choices and to create unambiguous categories and solutions to various problems, their ambition being to create order. However, according to Zygmunt Bauman, such an ambition is doomed to failure. Modernity is marked by ambivalence. Bauman describes the symptoms of this ambivalence in the following way:

> Ambivalence, the possibility of assigning an object or an event to more than one category, is a language-specific disorder: a failure of the naming (segregating) function that language is meant to perform. The main symptom of disorder is the acute discomfort we feel when we are unable to read the situation properly and to choose between alternative actions.
>
> (Bauman 1990: 1)

The solution to this complex of problems could be that people learn to accept and to deal with ambivalence. Paradoxically, the desire for order and the need to control nature and humankind – which are characteristic of modernity – lead to a constant intensification of the experience of ambivalence. Bauman also writes that: 'If modernity is about the production of order then ambivalence is *the waste of modernity*' (Bauman 1990: 15, original emphasis). The more that people try to exert a rational self-control or in some way try to create order in chaos, the more they are subject to the insecurity and uncertainty that constitute the down side of modernity.

Bauman distinguishes between two different approaches to ambivalence. On the one hand, people can do everything possible to reduce the level of ambivalence and create order in their lives. This approach is based on a denial of the fact that it is no longer possible to base a life on unambiguous and true alternatives. On the other hand, we can imagine an individual who accepts modernity and enjoys ambivalence. Such a person relinquishes all possibilities for forming a fairly stable identity and for being able to balance between order and chaos. Both of these approaches can be interpreted as flights from ambivalence. Most people tend to vacillate between these two strategies in their attempts to reach some kind of balance in their lives (Bauman 1993).

Traditions are essentially reproductions of routines, values and ideas that deal with how life should be lived and that are taken for granted. Although we find it difficult to accept such an unassailable and rigid outlook on the structure of everyday life, this does not imply that people have ceased to routinize and ritualize it. Routines and rituals help to create a feeling of ontological security. But such feelings of security can turn out to be deceptive. When routines no longer constitute a part of the reflexive self-identity project, but instead threaten people's ability to choose their lifestyles, they can be transformed into addiction and compulsion. Giddens discusses the relation between trust, compulsion and abstract societal systems in the following way:

> *Compulsiveness*, I want to argue, is *frozen trust*, commitment which has no object but is self-perpetuating. Addiction, to recapitulate, is anything we have to lie about: it is the obverse of that integrity which tradition once supplied and which all forms of trust also presume. A world of abstract systems, and potentially open lifestyle choices, for reasons already explained, demands active engagement. Trust, that is to say, is invested in the light of the selection of alternatives. When such alternatives become filtered out by unexplicated commitments – compulsions – trust devolves into simple repetitive urgency. Frozen trust blocks re-engagement with the abstract systems that have come to dominate the content of day-to-day life.
>
> (Giddens 1994: 91, original emphasis)

Conditions of addiction can be manifested in various ways: everything from alcoholism's destructive lifestyle to the workaholic's continuous pursuit of new signs of success. As long as the addiction is experienced as invigorating and affirming, it can dampen the anxiety created when people are always faced with the existential responsibility of managing their lives in the most sensible way possible.

Another way people can deal with this anxiety is to always be on the move and to never allow themselves to get 'trapped' in a relationship or a specific occupation. People who seek out the liquid aspects of life and who are skilled at seizing opportunities also avoid confronting their own ambivalence. However, such a lifestyle requires that individuals are clever at avoiding situations in which they must make choices that are crucial for their future. Thus, the individual must always be prepared to break away and move on to new destinations. Such a flexible and mobile lifestyle puts heavy demands on individuals' ability to deal with narcissistic infractions and the feelings of shame that are generated when their self-presentation is unsuccessful. This type of risk behaviour and play with the identity can lead both to great self-satisfaction and to resignation.

The tyranny of possibilities discussed by Arendt can be experienced both as stimulating and as a burden. In the end, it is a question of the individual's ability to deal with the uncertainty that characterizes our times. Although it is conceivable that the emotionology of late modernity revolves around the question of ambivalence and the various strategies used to deal with it, it is when we concretize and look more closely at how people with different prerequisites approach and develop this emotionology that we obtain a more subtle and modulated picture of the various forms of the late-modern identity.

The social psychology of late modernity's 'terrain'

All this theorizing about late-modern society has resulted in a new conceptual framework for the classical, social psychological discussions about roles, in- and out-groups, projection, avoidance, collective identities and so on. The fundamental discussions on society and individual that were carried out earlier within, for example, symbolic interactionism, are now treated by modernity theoreticians such as Giddens, Bauman and Beck. Through them, a large part of social psychology's system of ideas has been modernized and set into the context of a more general analysis of societal change.

Many of the concepts now used to analyse society are quite general in nature. Thus, they can only point out certain contemporary tendencies, and we must specify how they have been used in various analyses. The system of concepts presented in this chapter is based on a more general discussion of modernity. I have used the notions of different theoreticians to sketch out a framework that contains certain fundamental concepts and ideas. From this framework, we can then continue, adding additional tools of analysis, in order to arrive at an understanding of the nuances of day-to-day life.

The concepts presented above are part of a first concretization of the meaning of late modernity. But in order to analyse changes in everyday life and culture, we must tie this system of ideas to concepts such as class, gender, ethnicity, social and cultural context and so on. In this way, we can get gradually closer to the specific phenomenon we want to study, while not losing sight of our more overall theoretical framework. The concepts allow us to focus on the conditions for identity formation in late-modern society, but they are applicable at different levels. Certain concepts, for example, *individualization* and *risk environment*, are used when looking at historical change and the growth of a new type of society. And other concepts, for example, *style*, *addiction* and *narcissism*, focus on the individual's readiness and ability to work through and deal with the consequences of this overall process of change.

Working neither at the societal nor the individual level of analysis, Goffman was able to use his system of concepts in order to analyse phenomena such as total institutions, stigmatization of deviants and the presentation of the self. In a similar manner, Beck, in his book on the risk society, has been able to use large portions of the system of concepts reported above to analyse the question of the environment and changes in working life and the class society. The supply of social psychological concepts functions best when it is in contact with social reality. And then, new concepts and ideas are often generated as well.

Epilogue: the death of social psychology?

It is highly likely that many of the authors discussed in the theoretical part of this book would not call themselves social psychologists. Social psychology is often considered to be a micro theory, the purpose of which is primarily to focus on social interaction and not to tackle questions of societal and cultural conditions. But what unites the theoreticians and traditions dealt with in the previous chapters is that they all frame questions about the relation between the individual and society, and that they formulate a number of useful concepts and ideas. However, if it is indeed the case that many of them are opposed to being categorized as social psychologists, and if what we have called social psychology is more a central social scientific-philosophical perspective than a discipline in its own right, do we need to talk about social psychology at all? I think that we do, and I will try to support this opinion below.

There is a great need for reflection on personal identity. Discussions dealing with the question of identity fall in a theoretical area that has earlier been considered to be social psychology. Discussions of identity and the field of social psychology are largely characterized by a meta-theoretical level. Thus, we can use this type of theorizing to structure and organize our thoughts about various social and cultural phenomena. But if these reflections are to be useful, we must go further and apply them to different societal phenomena.

The concepts generated in social psychology are often general in nature. The advantage of concepts such as risk, trust, individuality, identity and so on, is that they build a bridge between the individual and societal level. However, this does not imply that they can be used automatically in different empirical studies. The formation of concepts constitutes one side of social psychological thought; the other side deals with contextualization and the analysis of social reality.

Social psychology is necessarily cross-disciplinary in character. Today, the leading theory development occurs in cross-disciplinary areas such as feminism, cultural studies, post-colonial studies and so on. In line with the increasing importance of the cultural level for identity formation in late modernity, it has also become more important to build a bridge between the humanities and the social sciences. This is also why, for example, cultural studies has taken such a central position in the development of theories about our age.

Social psychology is far from dead, but it has gradually become more diffuse in nature. The division between a psychologically versus sociologic-ally oriented social psychology has also meant that the more well-defined and coherent psychological tradition has taken over an increasingly large portion of the social psychological 'market'. With this book, my aim is to illustrate the strengths of the more sociologically oriented tradition and to remind readers of its existence. Even if the types of reflections contained in this book can be found in a number of other contexts, I think it is reason-able to argue for the retention of a theoretical field for social psychological thought.

In the following section, we will deal with some central themes in the field of social psychology. We will delve more deeply into certain lines of reason-ing, and my hope is that this will lead to further investigations of, and reflec-tions on, the relation between the individual and society in late modernity.

Note

1 Here we can name, among other things, Tönnie's distinction between *gemein-schaft* and *gesellschaft*, and Durkheim's *mechanical* and *organic solidarity*.

Part II Thematic perspectives

Late modernity and identity: an introduction

In contemporary social psychology, concepts such as role and self have been replaced by the notion of *identity*. Looking in the dictionary, we find that identity can have the following meanings: (1) exact likeness in nature or qualities; and (2) the condition of being oneself and not another (*Webster's Encyclopedic Dictionary* 1989). In social psychology, this relatively simple, original concept has gradually been filled with additional meaning and content. Because it has become more difficult for people to 'be themselves', that is, to 'tell' others who they really are, it has also become more problematic to define and delimit the concept of identity itself. One way to define a person's identity is to use certain social criteria such as class, sex, ethnicity, nationality, status, income; and/or psychological criteria such as personality type or aptitude. As long as we accept and agree on how such social and psychological factors should be defined, this approach works well. But today, determining these social and psychological identity criteria in an unambiguous way has become more difficult.

When we use the concept of identity, we are often talking about identity formation, that is about a *process* rather than a definite *position*. But it is difficult for people to 'identify themselves' straightforwardly and with confidence when the positions in which they have anchored their identities are now uncertain and unstable. This does not mean, however, that everything is drifting and that people have no opportunities to secure various identity claims. For example, even though the polar division into male and female has become increasingly difficult both to defend and maintain, it still shows remarkably great stability. The more people become aware of and affected by the insecurity of 'cultural and social homelessness', the more anxious they become to re-establish stable distinctions and identity positions.

For the most part, today's discussions of identity are about a *life project*. To be sure, the identity can be *temporarily* tied to different positions. By talking about how much they earn, their occupation, their age, where they live and so on, individuals can give others a picture of their social position. Such an identity story can either be quite clear or it can express subtle details including exclusive identity criteria such as taste and style. But even if people have great opportunities to tie their identities to more solid criteria and distinctions, a feeling of uncertainty often remains. For some people, this uncertainty constitutes a chance to explore 'who they really are' – beyond all social distinctions. The search for authenticity and heroic attempts to leave unique marks on history have been a strong driving force for mankind. At the same time, it is precisely this search and this constant calling into question of various truths that constitute a driving force in the post-traditional society and that accentuate the insecurity experienced by many.

The flipside of the search for authenticity and individuality is people's increased need to ontologize their identities. Today, the more masculinity is questioned, the more it is re-ritualized. Traditional masculine symbols, codes and identity positions are being used again, and we are even able to observe an increased nostalgia for these types of secured identities. However, these struggles and attempts to ontologize masculinity must be understood precisely in terms of the questioning of patriarchy and masculine hegemony. The contemporary identity is, thus, created in a social field where different types of identity claims and definitions of identity are at odds – where an ongoing struggle over how different identities should be defined is taking place. This field is characterized by both uncertainty and insecurity and by ongoing attempts to position different identities. The concept of identity is, thereby, used in order to talk about stability and change, security and insecurity, and process and position.

The relation between the popular and media culture, on the one hand, and identity, on the other, has become stronger and stronger in late-modern society. The mass media affect social interaction and identity formation in terms of both *form* and *content*. The mediazation of society has contributed to an extensive aesthetization of day-to-day life. The styles, symbolic expressions and body ideals circulating in the media also influence the creation of style and the aesthetization of everyday life. This is not done by creating completely identical impressions of life, of course, but by providing the material for identity formation and by setting an agenda for the forms of interaction. But the media not only affect form, they even affect content. Thoughts, ideas, information and knowledge circulate on a global market. Reception of this media content is marked by a number of contextual factors and structural conditions. Through their global distribution and proliferation, the media have a crucial effect on identity formation in late-modern society.

The thematic part of this book is divided into different themes. This is to allow the reader to delve more deeply into some of the questions discussed in Part I. In the thematic part we shall deal primarily with two main issues: identity and mediazation. In late-modern society, these two issues are, of course, intimately tied to one another.

In the first three chapters, some basic aspects of the late-modern identity will be considered. Questions of alienation and the unknown will cut straight across the discussion on modernity. Here we will touch on both the more general cultural and the more specific psychological alienation. In connection with this chapter, we will then discuss narcissism as an existential aspect of identity development. These chapters are concluded with a reflection on the relation between body and identity. Thereafter, the focus is on the mediazation of everyday life. We will discuss Joshua Meyrowitz's theories on the social psychological consequences of the media, as well as Stuart Hall's and a number of other authors' thoughts about how people, in general, approach media content. With reference to this theoretical discussion, we will look at a specific case study of the physicality of the 1990s. In the chapter entitled 'The global gym', changes in our views on the body and the shifts in the relation between masculinity and femininity will be analysed. In conclusion, we will return to the question of social psychology's mission and future.

5 Strangers and strangerhood

The stranger and the process of estrangement

> The stranger will thus not be considered here in the usual sense of the term, as the wanderer who comes today and stays tomorrow – the potential wanderer, so to speak, who, although he has gone no further, has not quite got over the freedom of coming and going. He is fixed within a certain spatial circle – or within a group whose boundaries are analogous to spatial boundaries – but his position within it is fundamentally affected by the fact that he does not belong in it initially and that he brings qualities into it that are not, and cannot be, indigenous to it.
>
> (Simmel [1908] 1981: 143)

'The Stranger', Simmel's essay from 1908, is an appropriate starting point for a discussion of the social psychology of estrangement. Simmel's potential wanderer – *the stranger* – is a reoccurring *Gestalt* in the social scientific as well as in fictional literature. The stranger is part of the group, while maintaining his or her freedom to leave it and move on. According to Simmel, the stranger is often a merchant who launches new products from foreign places and is involved in various types of monetary transactions. Simmel refers, among other things, to the history of the European Jews. The stranger is not a landowner, nor does he or she have deep roots in the culture in question. In this way, he or she embodies a special combination of distance and proximity, as well as of indifference and commitment.

According to Simmel, the stranger takes a relatively objective approach

to various questions. This objectivity consists of a special form of participation that is marked by a certain balance between distance and closeness.
The stranger is not bound by pre-established theses or opinions, but is
instead free to form his or her own opinion of various phenomena and
events. He or she is not caught up in familial relationships and other collective ties. This is why the stranger is often privy to secrets and other con-
fidences.

Although Simmel's point of departure was primarily the situation of the
Jews in Western Europe, his reasoning has a more general validity. There
are great similarities between the stranger and the psychotherapist. A psychotherapist is simultaneously close and distant. Within more psychoanalytically oriented psychotherapy, the role of the therapist is as empathetic
listener and witness to the client's stories and life history. Clients can use the
therapeutic relationship in order to work through traumatic memories and
to find new ways to relate to themselves. Thus, the psychotherapist can
either function as a receptacle for emotions or as an empathetic voice, but
never as a close friend or relation. The client does not see the therapist
during his or her time off, and the therapist does not discuss his or her
private life or problems with the client.

One of the prerequisites of the therapeutic relationship is that the therapist studies the client's most intimate and personal problems and memories,
but that the client never gets to know the therapist as a person with a personal life history. Engaging arguments about how the therapeutic relationship should be shaped have long taken place in the psychotherapeutic
literature. According to some, the psychotherapist should have a more
objective and analytical attitude towards the client, whereas others feel that
the therapist's personality has a great influence on the psychotherapeutic
process. It is commonly thought that the therapist should master both of
these approaches. Thus, it is a question of degrees of closeness and distance.

According to Simmel, even the most intimate relationships contain an
element of alienation. People are often attracted to one another on account
of similarities. Thus, what brings people together is often of more general
significance. Alienation arises when the feeling that the relationship is
unique disappears. This, according to Simmel, can occur even in love
relationships. Simmel writes:

> A skepticism regarding the intrinsic value of the relationship and its
> value for us adheres to the very thought that in this relation, after all,
> one is only fulfilling a general human destiny, that one has had an
> experience that has occurred a thousand times before, and that, if one
> had not accidentally met this precise person, someone else would have
> acquired the same meaning for us.
>
> (Simmel [1908] 1981: 153)

The stranger is often defined in terms of group characteristics, for example, ethnic background and nationality. Simmel's idea is that the stranger is constituted through a combination of a certain amount of closeness and a certain amount of distance. Of course, to some extent, these features are found in all relationships, but it is only when they occur in certain proportions and in a state of reciprocal tension that they give rise to the social category *the stranger*. A careful reading of Simmel shows that this category is related to long-term and overall processes in the culture. According to Simmel, modern culture is marked by an increasing gap between the subjective and the objective culture (Simmel [1911] 1981). The introduction of the money economy and the growth of the objective culture lead to increased alienation or strangerhood. There are great similarities between Simmel's descriptions of the stranger and his analysis of the tragedy of the culture. Simmel's discussion of the culture is tangential to Marx's analysis of the fetishistic quality of goods, but, in contrast to Marx, Simmel means that the culture as a whole is developing in a more and more abstract and objectivized direction:

> The fetishistic character which Marx attributed to economic objects in the epoch of commodity production is only a particularly modified instance of this general fate of the contents of our culture. These contents are subject to the paradox – and increasingly so as culture develops – that they are indeed created by human subjects and are meant for human subjects, but follow an immanent developmental logic in the intermediate form of objectivity which they take on at either side of these instances and thereby become alienated from both their origin and their purpose.
>
> (Simmel, in Frisby and Featherstone 1997: 70)

Whereas the social category *the stranger* is fairly limited to certain specific groups of individuals, *strangerhood* is more diffuse and is tied, to a greater degree, to more general social and cultural changes in society. What united the classic sociologists Simmel, Marx, Durkheim and Weber was that they all observed drastic transformations in the culture. They perceived the contemporary culture as being contradictory and fragmented. The use of concepts such as strangerhood, anomie and the iron cage bears witness to scepticism about these contemporary cultural changes. The individuals described by these classic sociologists became, in a way, freer and freer, while they were also subjected to more difficult strains and became increasingly alienated from the culture.

The increased alienation of the individual has not only been dealt with in sociology. Similar tendencies can be observed in psychology and literary works. In psychoanalysis, the human psyche is often described as an iceberg, in which large portions are unknown or hidden. Freud's development of psychoanalysis brought with it an increased awareness of the hidden and unconscious aspects of the personality and an increased alienation from the inner psychological landscape. The unconscious is unknown territory, and this territory represents a challenge and an invitation to science to explore and map its terrain. The early psychoanalysts' deep fascination with the unconscious is even found in the writings of authors such as Franz Kafka, Herman Hesse, Axel Sandemose, August Strindberg and Albert Camus, among others. We see a heightened awareness of the idea that what is often described as a double or 'shadow' – the dark side of the human psyche – represents, in reality, central mechanisms of identity formation and of adjustment to a more and more changeable culture.

In the following account, I will deal with different aspects of the increased alienation in modern culture. This alienation is related to an overall increase in reflexivity and an awareness of the complex processes that conspire in the creation of an identity. In the late-modern culture, the stranger no longer belongs to a separate social category, but instead characterizes the culture as a whole. The feeling of alienation is woven intimately together with the growth of a modern and differentiated societal system and with an increasingly abstract culture – that is, with modernity.

Alienation and the marginal man

> She pretended to be surprised. Home? You mean my homeland, my native country, and what kind of a country is that? She threw up her arms. In Taganrog, I did not attend the Orthodox Church, but the Catholic one. When *the pope* came down the church aisles, my school friends pulled away from me, *the Polack*. And in church the sermons were in French, so no one thought I belonged there. . . . When I came to Warsaw, they said: That little Moscowite. Russian accent and skin as dark as the Devil's. And then in Petersburg: *A young lady from Warsaw*. My husband took me on an excursion along the Volga – Well, Her Ladyship from the capital city, an artist. And now, in my later years, I have returned to Warsaw. Again, the same thing: Do you come from the borderlands or from Russia? Yes, it is immediately clear that you are a foreigner. And here as well, in Berlin, a stranger. Eine Fremde. Does this not make sense? Always and everywhere: a stranger.[1]
>
> (Kuncewiczowa 1976: 78, original emphasis)

Migration has occurred during all time periods. Different peoples have met under more or less peaceful circumstances. People have probably always discussed the similarities and differences between different groups. However, based on theories about, and empirical investigations of, people's everyday lives and identities, we can assume that the concept of the stranger has had different meanings at different points in time. According to Elias, increased individualization is intimately tied to the process of civilization (Elias 1991). People's increased awareness of their own individuality has even led to a more developed self-control, a feeling of being separate and an increased privatization of various expressions of emotion.

Many book titles have included the word *stranger*, and a large proportion of them are about encounters between people with different ethnic backgrounds or nationalities and feelings of non-inclusion during stays in foreign countries. We can name, for example, Maria Kuncewiczowa's *A Stranger* (1976), Margareta Kirk's *Always a Stranger* (1984) and Leslie Fiedler's *The Stranger in Shakespeare* (1972). People living abroad often feel as though they exist in two different worlds. Everett Stonequist has discussed this experience under the heading *The Marginal Man*.

The marginal man belongs simultaneously to two or more different cultures. This is a person who, as a result of, for example, emigration, education or marriage, leaves his culture of origin and enters a new one, but who fails to adjust himself satisfactorily to the new culture. He becomes marginalized and feels like an outsider in the new as well as the old culture. This double 'membership' leads to inner conflicts and ambivalence. These inner conflicts are often more pronounced if the individual's parents have different ethnic backgrounds or nationalities. In cases where the individual belongs to both a dominating and a dominated culture, this marginalization can be quite marked:

> Wherever there are cultural transitions and cultural conflicts there are marginal personalities. If the cultural differences are of major importance, if they include sharp contrasts in race, and if the social attitudes are hostile, the problem of the individual whose sentiments and career are bound up with both societies may well be acute. His dual connections will then be reflected in the type of life he leads, the nature of his achievements or failures, his conception of himself, and many of his social attitudes and aspirations. He will, in fact, be a kind of dual personality.
>
> (Stonequist 1937: 4)

In his description of the process that leads to marginalization, Stonequist distinguishes between three different phases: the initial phase, the crisis phase and the adjustment phase. During the *initial phase*, the individual has yet to reflect on what it means to belong to a specific ethnic group or nationality. Individuals begin to discover that they are treated differently because of their ethnicity, nationality or because they belong to another social group. They also become aware of the problems of super- and subordination and the stigmatization to which certain groups in society are subjected. During the *crisis phase*, individuals' self-image is transformed. They must develop a new self-image and deal with the inner conflict that has arisen as a result of marginalization. During this phase, the individual's regular habits and behaviours change drastically. The third phase signifies an adjustment to the existing circumstances and a *new orientation*. During this phase, the individual vacillates between hope and desperation. The difficulties he or she encounters can be so serious that adjustment becomes impossible. This often leads to an even deeper crisis. Because of marginalization, the individual is forced to live with constant ambivalence. 'In the case of the marginal man it is as if he were placed simultaneously between two looking-glasses, each presenting a sharply different image of himself' (Stonequist 1937: 145).

According to Stonequist, the marginal man – as opposed to others – often develops a reflexive attitude towards life. Thus, marginalization can have a positive effect on the individual's development. Through his knowledge of two or more cultures, the marginal man can gain a better understanding of, and feeling for, cultural differences. Modern society is marked by increased internationalization. Thus, according to Stonequist, having the ability to consider cultures from different points of view and to reflect on cultural diversity is positive. The individual, however, need not abandon his or her cultural origins. Instead, Stonequist emphasizes the importance of cultural origins and traditions, and he thinks that the cosmopolitan lacks a stable cultural foundation. The cosmopolitan lives on the surface, easily becoming blasé and bored, which creates an unstable personality.

Thus, as early as 1937, we can see in the analyses from *The Marginal Man* thoughts about how increased globalization affects the individual's identity. According to Stonequist, the marginal man is created in the big cities and in certain other environments that are characterized by frequent contact between people with different cultural backgrounds. He even uses the notion of *the marginal culture area*. In other words, there is a connection between long-term cultural change and the growth of the process of marginalization. Alienation is not necessarily bound to the level of the individual, but is instead primarily a cultural process affecting a great number of people. Modern society is marked by social and cultural differentiation, which results in, among other things, transformations in social identity. Role changing, identity games and cultural diversity have increasingly become a part of day-to-day life (Ebaugh 1988). The stranger is no longer only outside us, but also – and equally – a part of our identity.

Alienation and the decentring of the self

With the Freudian notion of the unconscious the involution of the strange in the psyche loses its pathological aspect and integrates within the assumed unity of human beings an *otherness* that is both biologic *and* symbolic and becomes an integral part of the *same*. Henceforth the foreigner is neither glorified as a secret *Volksgeist* nor banished as disruptive of rationalist urbanity. Uncanny, foreignness is within us: we are our own foreigners, we are divided.

(Kristeva 1991: 190, original emphasis)

With increased cultural complexity and individualization comes also greater reflexivity concerning the human psyche and the internal, hidden forces that are thought to control our conscious lives. Freud's explorations into the unconscious and psychoanalysis constituted a breakthrough for how we frame questions about the human psyche. Today, many of the concepts and theoretical angles that have developed in psychoanalysis are part of our everyday language. Modern humans have learned to live with their double and have, therefore, developed a certain humility before the hidden forces concealed in the psyche.

In 1914, Otto Rank – one of Freud's closest colleagues – wrote an essay entitled 'The Double'. This is a recurrent theme in fictional works and it even has some connection with what Jung calls the shadow. The double or the shadow expresses sides of the personality that are hidden and often frightening in nature. When the individual can no longer handle his or her inner conflicts and problems of guilt, a double is often created. The double embodies the internal aspects of the individual of which he or she is most afraid. When individuals are unable to recognize and integrate these aspects of their personality, the result is often a catastrophe.

The double is created in order to solve the individual's problems. It becomes, so to speak, the bearer of his or her fears and of the negative aspects of his or her personality. But creating a double is not without its risks. Doubles often turn against individuals and threaten their life. The inability to deal with this inner stranger leads to more or less premeditated suicide, as in Robert Louis Stevenson's *Dr Jekyll and Mr Hyde* and Oscar Wilde's *The Picture of Dorian Gray* (Wilde [1891] 1972).

The double can serve as a narcissistic confirmation of the self, a way to hold on to the image of oneself as young and beautiful or a longing for, and fascination with, that which remains the same. Striving for sameness can be interpreted in terms of a fear of death and change, a desperate attempt to maintain a self-image of eternal youth and constancy. In this context, Rank mentions Wilde's *The Picture of Dorian Gray*. Dorian Gray is a remarkably handsome and fascinating young man who has his portrait painted by a friend. Looking at the portrait, he declares that he would sell his soul to remain forever as handsome and as young as in the picture. The portrait seems to have supernatural powers. As the years go by, it gruesomely reflects Dorian's spiritual development. The portrait ages and is marked by Dorian's often cruel actions, while his youth remains intact. Even though he enjoys his carefree life and eternal youth, Dorian is horrified as he watches the portrait's transformations:

A feeling of pain crept over him, as he thought of the desecration that was in store for the fair face on the canvas. Once, in boyish mockery of Narcissus, he had kissed, or feigned to kiss, those painted lips that now smiled so cruelly at him. Morning after morning he had sat before the portrait, wondering at its beauty, almost enamoured of it, as it seemed to him at times. Was it to alter now with every mood to which he yielded? Was it to become a monstrous and loathsome thing, to be hidden away in a locked room, to be shut out from the sunlight that had so often touched to brighter gold the waving wonder of its hair? The pity of it! The pity of it!

(Wilde [1891] 1972: 88)

In the end, Dorian murders the man who painted the portrait and decides to destroy it. But by destroying the painting, Dorian takes his own life. He is found with a knife in his heart, his face haggard and revolting, while the portrait now depicts his former youth and beauty.

Another common theme that is intimately related to the construction of myths about the double involves stories about twins. In David Cronenberg's film *Dead Ringers* from 1988, both of the identical twins and gynaecologists Elliot and Beverly Mantle struggle to maintain a close relationship that is based on likeness. But when one of them suddenly falls in love with a beautiful woman, their relationship changes drastically. Beverly's love for Claire constitutes a threat to their intimate identification and striving for likeness. The brothers share a profound insanity that takes the upper hand and results in Beverly killing his brother on the operating table. After killing Elliot, Beverly makes a desperate attempt to reach Claire and re-enter the world, but he fails and finally returns to his brother. The film ends with the brothers lying naked, curled around each other on the floor. The attempt to differentiate was a failure and led instead to destructiveness and death.

The message that we are given again and again is that people must learn to live with their doubles. The shadow is an important part of the personality and it must be integrated and dealt with. It can even be thought of as an embodiment of the deep alienation, fear of death and struggle for wholeness that characterize contemporary man. The inability to accept inner complexity and dissociation often leads to suicide. Dorian Gray dies when he stabs his own portrait, Dr Jekyll dies in his struggle against the evil Mr Hyde and, in the end, the Mantle brothers could no longer harbour and share their insanity. The double is created in order to deal with people's inner insanity and fear of death. But its creation often has the opposite consequences. Rank writes: 'So it happens that the double, who personifies narcissistic self-love, becomes an unequivocal rival in sexual love; or else, originally created as a wish-defense against a dreaded eternal destruction, he reappears in superstition as the messenger of death' (Rank [1914] 1971: 35).

In a later paper, Rank again takes up the analysis of the double (Rank 1941). Originally, the myth was related to people's hopes for a life after death. The shadow and the double symbolized the immortal soul of humans. However, in modern Western society, the double has increasingly come to symbolize a threat to the individual's identity and life. Just as modern people's relation to death is marked by distance and denial, modern myth construction around the double is marked by terror before and fear of the inner, unknown world – of encountering one's fear of death on a deeper plane and of approaching the dark sides of one's personality.

Modern individuals have become more and more aware of the fact that they must deal with contradictions and ambivalence. The psychologization of society has contributed to the development of a reflexive approach to the self and the identity. Even though it is probably primarily members of the educated middle class who have worked on their identities through psychotherapy and various self-help courses, society on the whole has also become more psychological and reflexive. There is a plethora of books and magazines containing advice on how to take care of your children, how to develop your self-confidence, how to improve your marriage and so on. In general, we can observe an increasing awareness of the duality that characterizes the existential conditions of modern people. However, there are many ways to handle and address the ambivalence that this brings with it.

The eternal stranger

> Undecidables are all *neither/nor*, which is to say that they militate against the *either/or*. Their underdetermination is their potency: because they are nothing, they may be all. They put paid to the ordering power of the opposition, and so to the ordering power of narrators of the opposition. Oppositions enable knowledge and action; undecidables paralyze them. Undecidables brutally expose the artifice, the fragility, the sham of the most vital of separations. They bring the outside into the inside, and poison the comfort of order with suspicion of chaos. This is exactly what the strangers do.
> (Bauman 1990: 56, original emphasis)

> There are friends and enemies. And there are *strangers*.
> (Bauman 1990: 53, original emphasis)

Friends and enemies are one another's opposites. They are defined in relation to each other, in the same way as Hegel's *master* and *slave*. The stranger, on the other hand, rises in revolt against this antagonism. He or she is indeterminable, filled with contradictions and difficult to define. The stranger gives vent to a deep, intrinsic ambivalence in the culture and opens a language game that contains contradictions and undefinable terms.

The stranger constitutes a constant threat to social order and structure. This threat, however, was not as great in traditional society as it is in modern times. Then, strangers could always be categorized as either friends or enemies. But as they grow in number, problems with making such dualistic divisions arise. There are no clear guidelines for how one should relate to a stranger. According to Bauman, the nation-state constitutes an attempt to deal with the problem of the stranger. Through the definition of territories and attempts to determine who our friends and enemies are, the stranger is excluded from the community. According to Bauman, the nation-state is 'a religion of friendship'. Thus, attempts to stigmatize and exclude strangers are also attempts to avoid ambivalence and chaos.

According to Bauman, some groups more than others are characterized by strangerhood – for example, intellectuals – but an increased privatization of strangerhood can also be observed: all people experience alienation, at some time. To a certain degree, modern individuals are always strangers. They have no solid home base, but instead travel in time and space between different societal spheres, taking on many different roles. Strangerhood has become universal. But if everyone is a stranger, then perhaps no one is? Bauman thinks that strangerhood, like ambivalence, is inherent in postmodernity.

> It seems that in the world of universal ambivalence of strangerhood, the stranger is no more obsessed with the ambivalence of what is and the absoluteness of *what ought to be*. This is a new experience for the stranger. And since the stranger's experience is one most of us now share, this is also a new situation for the world. With such new experience, neither the stranger nor his world are likely to remain the same. But with what consequences?
>
> (Bauman 1990: 101, original emphasis)

In a diverse culture, everyone is directed towards their own existential loneliness or extraneousness. However, this extraneousness is becoming more privatized and less threatening (Kristeva 1991). A diverse culture does not assimilate strangers, it dissolves alienation itself by preventing the emergence of sharp divisions between different people. According to Kristeva, that which is alien exists within us – we are all strangers.

Both Bauman and Kristeva describe the more general meanings of alienation. To be sure, in the work of both authors we see a strong emphasis on people's feelings of homelessness and confusion, but this is partly seen as positive. Cultural changes that lead to increased diversity and a less suspicious attitude towards strangers – or to a complete dissolution of the category – are positive changes. If we live in a culture characterized by contradictions, ambivalence, plurality and a mixture of different codes, then identifying strangers is no longer necessary – because then we are all strangers. But does this mean that alienation only has positive sides?

In *The Stranger* by Albert Camus, published in 1942, we follow Mersault, a person made into a murderer by chance events. The book begins with Mersault attending his mother's funeral. He observes the funeral from the outside, feeling alienated from his dead mother and from the entire process. It is difficult for Mersault to involve himself with other people. When his girlfriend asks him if he wants to get married, he replies: '. . . it doesn't matter to me, we can do it if you want to'. Mersault tells his girlfriend that he does not love her, but that he can marry her anyway. And for that matter, he could marry practically anyone. His reply to the proposal leaves the girlfriend bewildered. Mersault watches everything from a distance and with indifference. Following the murder – which happens by chance – Mersault is subjected to a cross-examination during which he is asked about his childhood and his relationships. During the trial, he is presented as a completely impassive murderer. He has no objections to this presentation. The prosecutor claims that Mersault has removed himself from society and is incapable of understanding human feelings. When Mersault is sitting in his cell, waiting for his execution, he has his last revelation. He feels freed from the bonds of the earth and ready to be revived. At this moment, he experiences a sort of happiness and opens his mind to the world's kind indifference.

Camus' stranger is completely dissociated from the world around him, without roots and indifferent towards the people he meets. He is a totally alienated individual, lacking goals and hopes; a stranger with no affective ties to his surroundings, who is unable to develop feelings of that sort. Mersault is the total postmodern individual, who lives in a hallucinatory reality and observes the world with indifferent objectivity. He is not anchored to everyday life. This stranger does not express ambivalence, but rather cold indifference and impassivity. He is akin to the psychopathic murderer in Bret Easton Ellis' *American Psycho*.

The social psychology of the stranger

Simmel's essay on the stranger from 1908 has had a great influence on the social scientific literature dealing with the theme of the stranger (McLemore 1991). The unfortunate result of this is that the concept has been primarily associated with studies of marginality. Instead, the concept could have been used to look at various aspects of the phenomenon of the stranger and strangerhood. However, in defence of Simmel, we should note that his essay on the stranger has multiple meanings and that he discusses both the situation of the Jews in Europe and the specific alienation associated with their lifestyle and culture, as well as Western people's general feeling of alienation from the culture. In studying the literature in this area, we notice a swing from discussions of the specific alienation brought about by life in exile or social climbing, on the one hand, to more general discussions on modernity and alienation, on the other (see, for example, Harman 1988, Trondman 1994). Thus, the concept of the stranger is used differently by authors such as Bauman, Fiedler and Kristeva.

When we talk about different kinds of strangers, the discussion often involves an attempt to describe and analyse the differences and similarities between different social types. We can differentiate between the tourist, the immigrant and the social climber. Such examinations can take up how people react to different types of strangers and the different factors that affect degree of assimilation, status, identity and so on. Different dimensions can be used in order to determine which type of stranger we are looking at. Levine distinguishes between visitors, residents and members, but there are, of course, other possible categories (Levine 1985). In a study of the works of John Berger, Papastergiadis differentiates between two types of strangers: the *enlightened stranger* and the *seasonal worker* (Papastergiadis 1993). The enlightened stranger is welcomed by the new culture because he or she gives good advice and offers new know-how. This stranger is similar to a shaman. The seasonal worker, on the other hand, is forced to move from the village to the big city in order to make a living. He or she is torn, more and more, between two different cultures. In the end, they feel as removed from life in the village as they do from life in the big city. We can thus discern a spectrum of different types of strangers that are, in one way or another, coupled to modernity. But even though it is possible to talk about the social psychology of the stranger on a more general plane, it is also important to bring out the subtleties and different aspects of this social category.

In the contemporary social scientific literature, we can see a tendency towards using the concept of the stranger in studies of general cultural development and alienation. The positive aspects of such an overall cultural alienation are presented by Kristeva and Bauman. Through participation in different cultures and social spheres, individuals develop greater flexibility and the ability to adapt quickly to new situations. Qualities such as these are often rewarded in modern society. But, while there are positive aspects of alienation, there is also a dark side. In contrast to the enlightened and reflexive stranger, we also have the emotionally dulled and indifferent one. Our contemporary culture encompasses both aspects of strangerhood.

There are certain common social psychological bases for the phenomenon we have called alienation or strangerhood. However, it is important to again point out that there are differences between different types of strangerhood and different types of strangers. Even if modern people have become homeless and alienated from the culture in some general sense, such feelings and experiences are, of course, variously strong and have different effects on behaviour. Thus, it is important to distinguish between the overall alienation in the culture and the marginalization that exclusively affects certain vulnerable groups.

However, it is also important to analyse the relation between general and more specific alienation. According to Bauman, general alienation brings with it an increased feeling of responsibility for the other. In other words, the relationship to the other results in the taking of an ethical position. Here, the similarity to Lévinas' thoughts about the ethical relationship to the other is obvious. According to Lévinas, encounters with the other mean that the self becomes conscious of its ethical responsibilities. The self is infinitely responsible for its neighbour. Thus, the other causes an ethic movement in the psyche:

> It is this that is Desire: to burn with a fire other than the need that satiation is able to satisfy, to think beyond one's own thoughts. On account of this unassimilable surplus, on account of this beyond, we have called the relation that binds the Ego to the Neighbor the Idea of Infinity.
>
> (Lévinas [1967] 1993: 169)

But there is, of course, another side of the coin. In contemporary Western society, strangers are largely marginalized and excluded, treated as second-hand citizens or simply shut out from the circles of affluence and the 'good life'. Stricter rules of immigration are making it more and more difficult for strangers to be accepted. Although Western societies are becoming increasingly heterogeneous and mixed, the idea of a nation-state with strict boundaries and a homogeneous population still predominates.

In March 1999 – as I wrote – we were again forced to witness how people can be driven away from their homes and lives, and stripped of their identities. The ethnic cleansing and terror perpetrated in Kosovo leads our thoughts once again to Auschwitz and to the darker sides of modernity. The optimal situation in which encounters with the other bring about an ethical movement – a sense of responsibility and respect – is suddenly defunct. The stranger is no longer considered to be an asset, but instead a burden – a threat to order and stability.

The bureaucratic apparatuses so characteristic of modern societies, combined with technical sophistication and instrumental rationality, can lead to affluence, economic growth and so on. However, they can also be used to create a totalitarian state, where strangers are annihilated and ethnic cleansing is used as a means of constructing the perfect, well-ordered society. The problematic status of the stranger – a question Simmel raised at the beginning of the twentieth century – is still on the agenda, and it is intricately interwoven into the social psychology of modernity.

In the next chapter, we will take a closer look at contemporary identity and its vicissitudes. In particular we will focus on the question of narcissism.

Note

1 Translated by K.W.

6 Narcissism and the existential meeting with the other

Narcissism and the enigmatic face

The concept of *narcissism* or *narcissistic disorder* can be found in all conceivable and inconceivable contexts. There can hardly be another notion that has given so many contradictory interpretations and that constitutes such a complex hybrid. The innumerable attempts made to straighten out this tangle of approaches have often led to more confusion. Narcissism is used both to denote certain specific personality disorders in psychiatry and psychotherapy, and to describe a disintegrating society and culture in the context of cultural analyses. In everyday contexts, the term is used to describe people who are fixated on themselves and their own bodies. And narcissism and egoism are often treated as one and the same. In the psychoanalytic literature, a distinction is commonly made between 'pathological' and 'positive' narcissism. In contrast to pathological narcissism, the good variant is seen as a necessary condition for the development of a fairly stable self-image and feeling of self-esteem.[1]

The attempts made to identify and categorize the narcissistic personality have resulted in an objectivization of the concept. Instead of developing its dynamic possibilities, the notion of narcissism has been transformed into a descriptive, psychiatric tool and has, thereby, lost its critical potential. Also, discussions focusing on specific personality traits can easily switch tracks and end up as discussions on the narcissism of modern people (for example, the international discussion led by Lasch (1984, 1985) and Sennett ([1977] 1993), and in Sweden by Ramström (1991)). But the more we study the arguments concerning narcissism, the more we understand just how subtle and complex the concept is. Perhaps the point of such a concept should not be to make categories and stipulations, but rather to try to capture the aspects of life that are transitory and sublime – the foundation for the existential meeting with the other. However, if we use a one-dimensional approach in our attempts to establish the prerequisites for such a meeting, the result will be rough and simplistic analyses of modern people's identity. In the following, I will try to illustrate the importance of maintaining the dynamics that, at best, are attached to what we call narcissism.[2]

When Freud introduced the notion of narcissism, he also led psychoanalysis directly into a discourse on modernity.[3] In other, contemporary discussions in the area of cultural theory, notions such as the unconscious, the superego and instincts are seldom used, whereas the concept of narcissism occurs rather frequently. In an article from 1914 entitled 'Zur Einführung des Narzissmus' – when Freud talks about love and acknowledgement as things that are attained when there is a balance between the energy that is outwardly directed towards different 'objects' and the energy that comes back and charges the ego – he is also talking about the modern individual's identity. This individual is liberated from the collective and can only form their identity in encounters with other people; encounters that, because of the contingencies of modernity, rest on shaky ground. Freud's analytic work on the concept of narcissism is focused on the enigmatic meeting with the other:

> Further it is easy to observe that libidinal object-cathexis does not raise self-regard. The effect of dependence upon the loved object is to lower that feeling: a person in love is humble. A person who loves has, so to speak, forfeited a part of his narcissism, and it can only be replaced by his being loved. In all these respects self-regard seems to remain related to the narcissistic element in love.
>
> (Freud [1914] 1984: 93)

In our encounters with the other, we are all vulnerable. While this meeting means that we consume part of the energy needed in order to build up the self, as Kohut might have put it, it is also a necessary condition for our existence. When we look into the enigmatic face of the other, we are also looking at ourselves – or, more precisely, at the specific image of ourselves that is reflected in the other's eyes. Here, we discover who we are, but we are also forced to confront the fact that there are no simple answers to this question. At the same time, we allow the other to define us in their eyes and we, thereby, lose our sense of authenticity. Thus, the concept of narcissism is dynamic in nature and can be used to point out some of the contradictions on which modernity is based. In the following presentation, I will discuss a few of these themes. With my point of departure in psychoanalytic theory and the philosophical efforts of Emmanuel Lévinas and Zygmunt Bauman, I will try to elucidate their relevance to a theory of narcissism and modernity.

Between chaos and order

Whereas Oedipus is used to symbolize the establishment of law and order in society – what has been called *The law of the Father* in psychoanalytical theory – Narcissus is often a symbol of boundlessness and transcendence. Roughly speaking, we can say that those who worry about societal conditions and who see chaos wherever they look want to see a re-establishment of the law of the Father, whereas those who instead see oppression and a patriarchal order – directly related to that which is Oedipal – want to recognize the positive forces of unlimited narcissism. In discussions of such a polarization between the narcissistic and the Oedipal, primary narcissism is pitted against the Oedipal order. According to Freud, this early narcissism is characterized by an absence of limits and is often described as an oceanic condition that is dream-like in quality. It is possible to read an element of resistance against things Oedipal and the law of the Father into this primary narcissism. Given this, we might interpret secondary narcissism as an attempt to establish a functioning identity by attracting charges from external objects and creating a balance in the ego. Thus, from the chaos and boundlessness inherent in primary narcissism, an order is created in the ego through those identifications that help to charge it with energy.

In Lacan's description of this process, it is clearly a matter of a development from chaos to order (Lacan [1949] 1989). The individual first views himself or herself in his or her own mirror image and later in the eyes of others; through this process, the fragments of subjectivity that exist prior to the so-called mirror stage are melded into a more and more stable identity. While this development is necessary for the establishment of some type of stable identity, it also leads to alienation and the formation of what Winnicott might call a false self (Winnicott 1971, Phillips 1991). Although Lacan would likely take opposition to such an essentialistically coloured description of this development, he would probably agree with Freud's notion of a development from a more undifferentiated and objectless stage to the establishment of a more coherent self-identity.

By differentiating between primary and secondary narcissism, Freud creates two aims for the discussion on narcissism. On the one hand, we have a self-sufficient monad who has no contact with the outside world and whose body is charged with libidinal energy. This view of narcissism even includes notions of the oceanic experiences and dream-like conditions that dominate the infant's inner world. Recently, such descriptions of the infant have been called into question, but this image is still quite influential in terms of how psychoanalysts conceive of the beginning of human life.[4] Psychoanalytical descriptions of this early inner world are broad in scope. Here, we find everything from Melanie Klein's theory of the paranoid-schizoid condition to Kohut's self-psychological theory of deficiency. There is obviously a lack of consensus on how the condition of primary narcissism should be analysed.

On the other hand, we find more agreement in descriptions of secondary narcissism. The libido is drawn inward, away from the external world, in order to charge the self and create a starting point for development of the individual's identity. Most authors seem to think that this is a necessary developmental process. At this point, when libidinal energies are drawn inward and aimed at the self, there is a risk of pathology if the balance between the internal and external world is upset. When we talk about good narcissism, we mean the necessary charging of the self or, in other words, the basic need for acknowledgement from others and the need to become apparent.[5] Although there is agreement on the basic elements of this process, the positive or negative effects of such a development are varyingly stressed. I will return to this discussion in the section on the relationship between the true and the false self.

In the dynamic that takes place between primary and secondary narcissism, we again find several well-known notions. It is partly a matter of a developmental process that goes from chaos to order, and partly about a continuing individuation process in which individuals gradually free themselves from various dependencies and develop their own identity. Primary narcissism is an undifferentiated condition in which the boundary between subject and object has yet to be established. Such a liquid condition can be interpreted as a Utopia, where the entire body is charged with sexual energy and where everyone drifts in an experiential sphere that is dream-like and ecstatic. Primary narcissism can be understood as a justification for people's struggle to attain a greater unity – to be one with existence itself. But we can also be shocked by the psychotic world of experiences into which people are thrown and try to focus those forces that counteract a fragmentation of the ego and a dissolution of the identity.[6]

Secondary narcissism is characterized by an incipient differentiation of the ego and an individual who is grappling with the question: who am I? The title of one of Heinz Kohut's most well-known books, *The Restorations of the Self*, indicates that the identity is created actively (Kohut [1977] 1986). Here, he analyses the problems that can occur when individuals are not acknowledged by their parents and when they have no opportunities to vent their need to idealize certain people in their life. Just as primary narcissism can be interpreted in negative as well as positive terms, secondary narcissism can be related to both self-development and alienation.

The point of departure of a dynamic conception of narcissism is the balance between chaos and order and between fragmentation and individuality – a balance that constitutes a precondition for the development of the individual's identity. The charging or acknowledgement of the ego takes place in an interplay with the other. This is a dynamic and subtle process that includes risks of deficiency and of disruption of the balance between the ego and the surrounding world.

Individuality and homelessness

According to some theoreticians, narcissism is a developmental stage that is passed through on the way to mature genital sexuality. However, such an approach to narcissism could lead to bypassing and ignoring the dynamic discussed in this chapter. The individuality and distinctive character a person might achieve during their life are chimerical and temporary in nature. Individuals continuously vacillate between the desire to achieve a larger context – whether it be a collective, a group or a religious community – and the desire to cultivate their own individuality. This dualism is not without its problems. In her article on 'The Dual Orientation of Narcissism', Lou Andreas-Salomé describes an episode from her childhood that caused her to experience herself as rootless and strange:

> It concerned an impression I had of my own reflection in the mirror. With a sudden unheralded awareness, I saw my own existence separate from that of all others. It was nothing in my appearance – such as being less pretty than I had imagined, – nor guilt aroused by the sin of doubt. It was rather the fact of standing forth as a bounded individual that left me homeless and impoverished, – as if hitherto I had found a welcome place for myself as part of everyone and everything.
>
> (Andreas-Salomé [1921] 1962: 7)

This transition from a state of rest and self-sufficiency to the individuated person's feeling of homelessness is a central theme in the discussion on narcissism. This theme also intersects the discussion on modernity. In Peter Berger's classic book *The Homeless Mind*, it is precisely this feeling of rootlessness and alienation that constitutes the very essence of the experience of modernity (Berger *et al.* 1973). Thus, the construction of the concepts of primary and secondary narcissism corresponds in many ways to the construction of the story of modernity – a story in which individuals are thrown out into the world to make their fortune. Freud never explored this side of the concept, but in spite of this we find that many of his formulations point towards just such a discourse on modernity.

The alienation from oneself that modern humans have been forced to deal with is partly the result of the increased reflexivity that marks modernity (Ziehe 1989, Giddens 1991). The demand for reflexivity and individuality is also a force that drives people to leave a state of narcissistic self-sufficiency and to allow themselves to be constantly called into question. A person who has successfully balanced their narcissism in relation to the rest of the world can also accept those feelings of ambivalence and inadequacy that are a consequence of a modern way of life. If the ego is threatened and the individual draws in his or her 'charges' from the external world in order to instead feed his or her own narcissism, a condition of self-sufficiency is created. This individual does not want anything to upset their introverted narcissism. And it becomes impossible to deal with feelings of ambivalence and other threats to the self-image. When such a state develops in a direction that is negative for the individual, we can talk about a 'narcissistic disorder'.

One prerequisite for the individual's development and individuation is a good narcissistic balance. If there is only enough energy to charge the ego – and nothing left to be directed outwardly – the result is a pathological condition. In modern society, however, the boundaries between such a pathology and other expressions of imbalance in the individual's 'narcissistic economy' are floating. Also, such imbalances can be expressed in many different ways. But what unites them is people's fear of, and difficulties with, the alienation they face and the lifelong challenge inherent in vacillating between feelings of belonging and acknowledgement, on the one hand, and experiences of exclusion and alienation, on the other.

The true and the false self

The formation of an identity partly involves the incorporation of others' outlook on the individual and partly the search for authenticity. When Lacan describes this identity process, he focuses primarily on the creation of what Winnicott might call the 'false self'. The mirror image that serves as the starting point for identity formation results in a false feeling of order and coherence. According to Lacan, this mirroring process gives the child the false promise of a unified identity. But whereas Lacan's version of this mirroring in the face of the other is centred on the alienating effects of the process, Winnicott thinks that what children see in the mirror is determined by their specific experiences of the mother's face. Not being acknowledged by the mother is like not existing. According to Winnicott, the mother is the constitutive witness to the 'true self'.

Winnicott's version of the mirror phase deals with the intricate interplay between the true and the false self. If the parents have been completely incapable of responding appropriately to the child's spontaneous gestures and needs, the child is then forced to adapt to their needs instead of developing a feeling for its own rudimentary self and the needs of the self. Winnicott distinguishes between different degrees of a false self, where the most extreme case is when it is hardly possible to discern the true from the false self. This corresponds to Lacan's description of the mirror phase. However, it is often possible to discern a dialectic between the true and the false self. Here, we are able to focus on the subtle boundary between a person's

adaptive ability to adjust and be sensitive to signals from his or her surroundings, on the one hand, and the unreal feelings and absence of creativity
and spontaneity that characterize the thoroughly false self.

Of course, postulating the existence of a true self is not completely
unproblematic. If differentiating between a good and a pathological narcissism is to be at all reasonable, we must use a conception that allows us to
capture people's experiences of authenticity or alienation. There is, naturally, never *one* true depiction of a person or an ultimate truth about an
individual's life, but this does not mean that we cannot discuss how people
oscillate between exaggerated adaptation to external demands and the
search for their own viewpoints. Winnicott's notions do not require any type
of essentialism, but can instead be used to develop our thoughts about
people's construction of their own identities.

In the area of cultural theory, the discussion on contemporary people's identity is often focused on the openness, plasticity and contingency that characterize the culture. In a culture that offers a large assortment of lifestyles and
that allows people to find their own identities, individuals must develop an
ability to read their environment in a flexible way and to deftly adjust to new
milieux and requirements. In such a context, narcissistic problems are
brought to the fore – problems of being able to oscillate between a true and
a false self without losing faith in oneself and one's own identity project.

In late-modern society, the individual's self-esteem is subject to considerable strains. Many social milieux can be described as *critical* in that they
require of the individual a great aptitude for adjustment and an adequate
presentation of the ego (Goffman 1967). In contexts such as these, there is
a risk that the individual will develop a false self as protection, and in order
to retain some form of self-esteem and feeling of authenticity.

Ethics and infinity

Much of psychoanalytic theory deals with people's encounter with the
Father (Lacan), that is with the Oedipal drama and the establishment of the
law of the Father. Although authors such as Kohut and Winnicott have tried
to analyse the fundamental meeting with the other, ideas about the existential aspects of this meeting are largely lacking. This meeting with the other
is not only a matter of people's need for acknowledgement and the neces-
sity of charging the ego, but it is also a matter of distinguishing between
the subject and the other, and of ethics. Lou Andreas-Salomé's depiction of
Narcissus is different from that advocated by Freud. To a greater extent
than Freud, she stresses the existential meeting with the other:

> Bear in mind that the Narcissus of legend gazed, not at a man-made
> mirror, but at the mirror of Nature. Perhaps it was not just himself that

he beheld in the mirror, but himself as if he were still All: would he not otherwise have fled from the image, instead of lingering before it? And does not melancholy dwell next to enchantment upon his face? Only the poet can make a whole picture of this unity of joy and sorrow, departure from self and absorption in self, devotion and self-assertion.

(Andreas-Salomé [1921] 1962: 9)

Taking the ideas of Lévinas and Bauman as my point of departure, I will now try to convey the notion that we – instead of getting caught up in analyses of narcissism that deal only with individuals' need for confirmation and their construction of imaginary images – should focus on the individual's desire to get to know the other, as well as on the ethical aspects of this process. People's ability to lose themselves and become part of collective processes is not exclusively a bad thing, but implies instead a potential for greater humility and respect for life. The capacity for temporarily losing one's ego is tied to the boundlessness of primary narcissism.

Lévinas' interest is in the dialectical interplay between the ego and the other. In concrete encounters with other people, face-to-face, individuals are made aware of their own solitude. Such encounters also bring to the fore questions of people's eternal struggle to attain greater wholeness: the search for the other. But the other will always be a mystery to us; as soon as we begin to treat him or her like an object or to see love as a form of fusion between two people, we have removed ourselves from that which makes us human. The pathos of love lies in the invincible duality between beings. It is a relationship to that which is always fleeting (Lévinas [1948] 1992). Lévinas sees the foundation of the ethical meeting between two people in the caress and in the approach to the other's face. While the encounter with the other makes us aware of our own absolute solitude, an ethical movement is also generated in the psyche; the ego loses its sovereign self-identification and discovers its responsibility for the other and its relation to what Lévinas calls the Idea of Infinity. Thus, we are now dealing with a meeting with something we can never put into words – a meeting with the other (Kemp 1992).

What I want to try to get a grip on here is Lévinas' analysis of the relation between the meeting with a concrete individual, face-to-face, and people's desire to go beyond what exists and to seek an answer to the question of the meaning of life. Lévinas writes: 'The relationship to the Neighbor puts me in question, empties me unceasingly of myself, in that it, in this way, is always discovering new assets in me. I did not know I was so rich, but I no longer have the right to retain anything' (Lévinas [1967] 1993: 165). When a person is mirrored in the face of the other, it is not only a matter of seeking acknowledgement of the ego, but also a matter of desiring to transcend the bodily existence and take part in the Idea of Infinity. Just as Lou Andreas-Salomé describes people's eternal oscillation between individuality and a wish to be part of a larger, all-encompassing whole, Lévinas explores the fundamental duality that is a part of people's existential condition. And this is also the central dynamic in the dialectic between primary and secondary narcissism.

While modern individuals strive to develop their individuality and to elevate their own feelings and thoughts to centre-of-the-universe status, they are reminded again and again that they are part of a larger social context: a family, a collective or some other social group. The ambivalence that characterizes this condition – of vacillation between fixation on one's own ego and a constant calling into question of the self – is part of modern individuals' terms of existence. In contemporary society, the accentuation of this complex of problems has kept pace with what is usually called the process of individualization and the development of the 'cult of the individual'.

Although Lévinas deals indirectly with questions of modernity and identity, he fails to discuss how modern individuals handle the 'homelessness' and alienation that are a consequence of modernity. In this case, we can turn to the sociologist Bauman, who, in several books, has touched on the ambivalence and disorientation that mark contemporary individuals' life situation (Bauman 1993, 1995). According to Lévinas, ethical relationships are based on people's readiness to accept the fact that they are separate from the other and that they can never attain absolute unity with another person. In other words, recognition of differences is of central importance for the establishment of an ethical relationship.

It would seem that the modern individual wants to abolish differences and avoid feelings of ambivalence. However, according to Bauman, avoidance of such feelings is impossible; it is instead the case that this state of confusion and dissociation has become a primary ingredient in modern life. People, of course, try to manage these feelings in different ways. In *Postmodern Ethics* – a book based largely on Lévinas' philosophy – Bauman distinguishes between two ways of relating to the other. Among other things, he talks about *fixation*, which means that people try to avoid uncertainties and ambivalences in various relationships by routinizing these relationships and creating rules for how they should approach the other. With regard to this strategy, Bauman writes:

> Duty replaces love, as the comfortably familiar routine replaces frantic effort and adventure. Love is an uphill struggle, duty is effortless – when practised consistently, it turns into habit . . . This is a tranquil unpleasantness, one that breeds sadness, but does not spur into action. The unpleasantness of a cemetery, one is tempted to say. Indeed, duty is the death of love – of its splendours as well as its torments . . .
>
> (Bauman 1993: 99ff)

But the other strategy – of accepting the *liquid*, of leaving relationships when they begin to get boring or stop giving dividends – is just as destructive. This type of relationship is based on the premise that life is an adventure – which never ends.

Both of these strategies lack an ethical dimension – the other is someone to be manipulated and controlled. In other words, the individual waives his or her responsibility for the other. According to Bauman, in order to create the preconditions for an ethical relationship with the other, we must learn to live with ambivalence. We cannot run from the freedom we are offered; such a flight would connect us inexorably with modernity's destructive forces. Respect for the other is a central theme for both Lévinas and Bauman.

As I see it, what we call narcissism is actually a matter of fundamental aspects of the meeting with the other; of the constant vacillation between individuality and the desire to join the collective; of our mortality and our responsibility for the other. And similarly, what are often called 'narcissistic pathologies' actually concern people's difficulties in dealing with the existential, psychological and cultural prerequisites for the development of a self. But this narcissistic dynamic is not only about the problems inherent in the meeting with the other; it is also about the possibility of developing an ethical relationship with the other. Just as it is necessary – in a psychological sense – to develop a good narcissism, a charging and acknowledgement of the ego, in the meeting with the other it is also important to temporarily lose the ego, only to return to it later. It is important to be able to swing between participation and individuality. Bauman's strategies – fixation and acceptance of the liquid – constitute attempts to avoid confrontations with uncertainty and ambivalence.

Narcissism and existence

The discussion on narcissism includes many simplifications and tendencies towards reifying the concept. I have tried to show how what we call narcissism is created in an interplay between different factors. The concept is dynamic in nature and presupposes an analysis of the dialectic between chaos/order, individuality/fragmentation, the false and the true self, and so on. Narcissism is not a static condition, but is instead an ongoing process that forms the existential basis for contemporary individuals' identity formation.

The discussion on narcissism has been made more difficult by the division into primary and secondary narcissism. It is almost as though two lines of argument have been created; one focused on the dissolution of boundaries, cultural disintegration and transcendence, and the other on the formation of a stable identity. It is for this reason analyses of, and questions related to, the relation between these two stages are lacking. Roughly speaking, we can see two tendencies in the interpretation of narcissism and culture; on the one hand, we have an emphasis on the state of dissolution that originates from primary narcissism and that is followed by a growing feeling of estrangement and alienation, and, on the other hand, we have discussions on primary nar-cissism as something positive – becoming a part of the whole in order to later reconnect to the ego – that with time leads to a fairly stable identity and feeling of self-esteem. In other words, different analyses of the process of nar-cissistic development are associated with different symbolic meanings.

Rather than fastening on a one-sided analysis of narcissism, I would like to propose that we try to cultivate the dynamic qualities of this concept. People's identity is formed in the continuous interplay between dissolution of boundaries and creation of order, between the search for authenticity and the playing of roles, and between individualization and fragmentation. When we study this process, it is important to talk about narcissism as a central aspect of the process leading to the formation of an identity. Nar-cissism is the psychological energy that – depending on how we direct and manage it – forms the basis for how we approach the other. In talking about narcissism, we touch on people's capacity to feel full of, or lacking in, strength and energy. The longing to lose oneself in the other is based on con-fidence in the surrounding world, a feeling of wanting to be filled with posi-tive identifications. Fear of fragmentation and dissolution is based on a lack of such confidence, a fear of being filled with negative identifications and charged with demanding and consuming inner objects. Just as there is a sym-bolic language built up around the oral, the anal and the Oedipal, there is also a world of symbols tied to narcissism. This symbolic language is well suited to the discourse on modernity, in which notions such as homeless-ness, identity, fragmentation, individuality and order versus chaos are used in order to illustrate a contemporary social and cultural landscape.

Thus, it is clear that the story of narcissism is not only about the patholo-gies of our time or a psychiatric condition. The concept has a much broader meaning. It encompasses everything from the foundations of our being to the creation of a fairly stable identity and self-opinion. The discussion on nar-cissism is often related to a more general view on culture. This is, of course, a function of the division of the concept into primary and secondary narcis-sism. In Freud's *Beyond the Pleasure Principle*, primary narcissism takes on an almost mythical quality. As I see it, this is related to the nirvana principle and the death instinct, that is, to the dissolution of the ego (Freud [1920] 1995). Here, life and death stand face-to-face, and Freud's thoughts are, thereby, tangential to the discussion led by, for example, Nietzsche on Apollo's struggle against the Dionysian forces in life, and also tangential to the entire discussion on culture that is focused on the relation between the disintegrative and constructive forces in society and culture. Whereas the dis-cussion on primary narcissism can be coupled to such existential forces in life, discussions on people's search for authenticity and an identity can begin with the concept of secondary narcissism. Thus, the notion of narcissism will certainly remain a dynamic tool in our attempts to approach and understand the consequences of modernity.

When Christopher Lasch wrote his influential book *The Culture of Narcissism* (1985), his ideas rested heavily on an oversimplified notion of narcissism. Lasch identified a number of problematic features of contemporary culture and related all of them to 'narcissism'. According to Lasch, the end of the patriarchal society and the beginning of the mass media-saturated society marked the start of a new era – of a new shallow society and a new social character: the narcissistic personality. Two factors in combination – the loss of the stable guidance and impact of the patriarchal father and the accentuated influence of the mass media – led to the development of a fragmented, unattached and weak-minded individual, according to Lasch.

Of course, using the notion of narcissism in this way – as a tool for a social conservative critique of society and culture – is deeply problematic. The concept of narcissism introduced in this chapter takes into consideration the ambivalent nature of modernity and of contemporary identities. It takes us directly to the forefront of contemporary identity without exaggerating the unstable or stable, fragmented or coherent, 'true' or 'false' aspects of it. This use of the concept makes it easier to approach and analyse different societal phenomena in their full diversity, without portraying people as cultural dopes who are easily influenced and manipulated by the mass media, authoritarian leaders and so on.

In the next chapter, we will deal with the questions of narcissism and contemporary identity in a somewhat different way, by looking more closely at the social psychology of the body.

Notes

1 The present use of the word pathology denotes the individual's own experience of suffering and 'illness'.
2 In Sweden, there has long been a discussion of how narcissism can be understood as a dynamic concept – see Alvesson (1989), Fornäs (1991), Johansson (1994, 1995a,b,c, 1996a) and Sernhede (1997).
3 Freud has touched on narcissism in a number of papers (see, for example, Freud [1914] 1984, [1917] 1984 and [1923] 1984). See also, Frimodt (1985) and Laplance and Pontalis ([1967] 1988).
4 In an earlier paper, I discuss Stern's theory of infant development. This theory can be viewed as a sharp criticism of the idea of primary narcissism (Johansson 1995b).
5 In his book on narcissism, Sigrell (1994) takes up Tove Jansson's story about the invisible child as a good example of this dynamic.
6 These viewpoints are held by different authors. Herbert Marcuse (1955) has chosen to recognize early narcissism and the potential for resistance found in the pre-Oedipal body and sexuality; Lou Andreas-Salomé has discussed the existential dimension of narcissism (Andreas-Salomé, [1921] 1962, 1964 and 1972); and finally, Kernberg ([1975] 1983) has discussed narcissism as a pathological condition.

7 The social psychology of the body

The time of the body

During the 1990s, the corpus of literature dealing in one way or another with how we look at the body in late-modern society has grown considerably. Although a more scientifically oriented interest in the human body is not an entirely new phenomenon, we can, today, clearly observe an increased interest in people's physical existence. Explanations for how this theoretical and empirical 'field of research' has come about can be found both *within* and *outside* the sciences.

In terms of the former, we can see increased differentiation and specialization in contemporary social sciences. Many authors' scientific works that are today categorized as belonging to the discourse on the body were earlier placed under the heading civilization theory, general sociological theory and feminist research. One of the driving forces behind the growth of the sociology of the body is the English sociologist Bryan S. Turner. In a number of books, Turner has actively taken part in the development of a discourse on the body (for example, Turner 1984, 1987, 1992). Most of his books could also be classified under the heading medical sociology, but his intention is to contribute to a more general discussion on the body in late-modern society.

Turner discusses phenomena such as anorexia, the phenomenology of the body, gender and the body, and consumption and the body. Together with the group of English cultural sociologists who started the journal and book series *Theory, Culture & Society*, and later *Body & Society*, he has also helped to attract a number of researchers to the theme body and society. The result of this has been several interesting articles, books and anthologies on the body. The anthology *The Body: Social Process and Cultural Theory* was germinal in this regard (Featherstone *et al.* 1991a).

In explaining this increased interest in the body from outside the sciences, it is difficult to make any definite statements. However, we can imagine that the following factors have played a role in this development: (1) the increased focus on the youthful, beautiful body in the mass media and advertisements; (2) the rising interest in 'youthfulness'; and (3) the development of a number of body techniques, for example, methods of dieting, surgery and training methods such as body building and aerobics. These phenomena are intimately interrelated. The mass media's images of young, beautiful and successful people have affected a larger and larger group of people of different ages, and have created among them a longing for youthfulness. Today we have several well-developed and refined body techniques that can be used to attain the particular ideal of interest. At this point, we may want to stop and wonder: what is it that causes people in the social sciences, humanities, the art world, film, television, advertising and so on to become interested in the body and physicality?

The growth of the discourse on the body is intimately tied to several of the most central theoretical discourses taking place during the 1990s. In this case, I mean feminism, discussions on postmodernity, the cultural studies tradition, cultural sociology and psychoanalysis. Within these different traditions, discussions on the body and culture are overlapping and largely complementary, but are not identical.

In the area of feminism, there has long been an interest in the body and physicality. We find several classic works here, for example, Julia Kristeva's *Powers of Horror. An Essay on Abjection* (1982), Frigga Haug's *Female Sexualization* (1992) and Judith Butler's *Gender Trouble: Feminism and the Subversion of Identity* (1990). One article that has had a great impact on this discussion is Donna Haraway's 'A Manifesto for Cyborgs', in which the cyborg is used metaphorically to focus on the boundaries between masculinity and femininity (Haraway 1990). In this context, we should also name the literature that deals with masculinity and the body. An early work within this tradition is Klaus Theweleit's *Male Fantasies* (1995).

Almost all of the books mentioned above can be classified under the heading postmodern theory. This criticism of the centred subject and the acceptance of the dissolution of various boundaries have greatly influenced the discussion on the body. One book in which this discussion is well summarized is Mike Featherstone's *Consumer Culture and Postmodernism*. Here we find a critical sociological treatment of theories of the body and consumption (Featherstone 1991b). This cultural sociological work has been germinal to much of the Anglo-Saxon theory-building that is focused on the body and society.

In the cultural studies tradition, researchers have explored the relation between advertising, aesthetics, youth, music and so on, and the body. We find an early interest in these issues within British cultural studies. Discussions on youth, style and taste within the so-called Birmingham school are largely tangential to today's deliberations on the body. A good example is Dick Hebdige's book about punk-rockers, *Subculture: The Meaning of Style* (1979), which deals with young people's continuous creation of new stylistic and bodily means of expression. Two books providing a good presentation of the more general cultural sociological discussion are Pasi Falk's *The Consuming Body* (1994) and Cris Shilling's *The Body and Social Theory* (1993). Falk and Shilling's discussions of the relation between the body and society are more ontological in nature.

In the following sections, I will discuss several areas of interest in this field. The classic debate of actor versus structure is constantly at hand in theories of the body. The focus is either on the tendency for people to be subordinated in various ways and on how societal oppression and disciplinization are inscribed in the body, or on theories of how desire and physicality are linked to consumption and advertising. There is a clear tendency in the literature to overemphasize the structural aspects and ignore the actor.

I will continue by exploring the social scientific discussion on the body's importance in the process of structuring society. One of my points of departure is Giddens' theory on the duality of structures. Finally, I will return to the issue of the body's role – its 'to be' or 'not to be' – in social scientific discussion.

Body, discipline and resistance

In sociology, there has long been an interest in studies of how social oppression and power structures are engraved in the physical corpus of people. Thus, by studying how the body and its disciplinization are viewed, we can make more general inferences about the conditions of power in society.

Early social scientific discussions on the body and society took place primarily in the areas of anthropology and sociology. Here, Marcel Mauss' paper on body techniques, 'The Notion of Body Techniques', is central (Mauss [1959] 1979). In this short text, Mauss shows us the connection between body techniques and societal systems. He begins this essay by discussing his own swimming technique, and then continues to show how different societies foster different body techniques. He writes:

> In my day swimmers thought of themselves as a kind of steamboat. It was stupid, but in fact I still do this: I cannot get rid of my technique. Here then we have a specific technique of the body, a gymnastic art perfected in our own day.
>
> (Mauss [1959] 1979: 99)

Although this essay is central to the continued discussion on body techniques, a treatment of the actor and the body is largely lacking. The primary purpose of the essay is to classify various body techniques.

In Mary Douglas' classic work *Purity and Danger*, we find a discussion on the connection between bodily and societal limits (Douglas 1970). In short, Douglas thinks that there is a correspondence between, on the one hand, the establishment of bodily limits – which occurs through people's expressions of disgust, loathing and fear of filth – and, on the other hand, societal order. The struggle against filth is also a struggle against those who refuse to conform to the societal order and who, thereby, threaten this order.

One important work that was rediscovered during the 1970s is Norbert Elias' influential theory of the so-called process of civilization (Elias [1939] 1989). Douglas and Elias' theories correspond closely on several points. Elias describes a development from antiquity to modern society, in which the human body is gradually disciplinized and physicality is made taboo and subordinated to normative regulation. The increased need for personal integrity and delimitation from the surroundings is partly related to increased individualization and partly to the establishment of a new societal order, characterized by the formation of demarcated nation-states (for a criticism of Elias, see Duerr) (Duerr [1987] 1994).

In terms of contemporary discussions on the body and society, the most influential ideas probably come from the French philosopher Michel Foucault. In his books on prison and human sexuality, Foucault has shown how societal power structures are concretely and materially expressed in terms of bodily disciplinization (Foucault 1978, 1979, 1985 and 1986). Societal super- and subordination are inscribed, so to speak, in human bodies. In line with Elias, Foucault discusses how traditional society's external control over people was transformed into the internalized control that marks modern society.

In many ways, Pierre Bourdieu is a good representative of sociologically oriented discussions on the body and society. In *Distinction*, he develops a theory of the connection between status, taste, style and body (Bourdieu 1984). He shows quite convincingly how status and power relations are expressed in terms of different styles and tastes as well as different bodies. From early in life, various codes and bodily expressions are already engraved in an individual's *habitus*. In the struggle to achieve a status position in society, these codes and expressions are either a help or a hindrance. Using considerable detail, Bourdieu shows us how the connection between status, style and body is a manifestation of an overall societal order.

The theoreticians mentioned above have all played an important role in the development of a theoretical discourse on the body. They have all tried to understand the relation between body and society. However, according to Turner, these theoreticians are quite separate from the rest of social science, from which physicality is conspicuously absent. Therefore, during

Figure 1   Typology of the relation between body, society and illness (from Bryan S. Turner 1984)

	Populations	*Bodies*	
Time	Reproduction Malthus Onanism	Restraint Weber Hysteria	**Internal**
Space	Regulation Rousseau Phobia	Representation Goffman Anorexia	**External**

the 1980s and 1990s, a number of sociologists have tried to collect and integrate the various deliberations on the body and society. In order to help the reader and provide a sort of introduction to this far-reaching discussion, I will give an account of Turner and Frank's (1991) independent attempts to construct typologies of different theories related to the body and society.

In his examination of this topic, Turner starts with Hobbes' question: How is society possible? Thus, he focuses on how a specific societal order is created via disciplinization of the body (Turner 1984). As a foundation for such a discussion, he develops a typology that results in four different ideal types: *reproduction, asceticism, control* and *representation*. The purpose of Turner's typology is to add to the development of Foucault's discussion on the relation between the illnesses of the citizens, on the one hand, and political and ideological discourses, on the other (see Figure 1).

One theoretician who has probably influenced societal debates on population growth more than others is Thomas Malthus. According to Malthus, there are two primary driving forces that dominate people's existence: hunger and sexual passion. When people's sexual needs lead to increased population growth, which in turn leads to famine and poverty, the desires of the masses must be controlled through the exertion of moral influences. Thus, the solution to the problem is to encourage celibacy and delayed gratification of instinctual drives. Sexual excesses should wait until marriage, and marriage should occur only if the financial situation allows. Delayed gratification also constitutes a strong argument against masturbation, which is considered to imply an acceptance of lust and to be non-productive and morally reprehensible.

Max Weber's thesis on Protestant ethics and the spirit of capitalism has coloured much of the discussion on the bourgeois personality. The ascetic deportment that was practised in the type of Protestantism examined by Weber contributed to the creation of a social character marked by self-discipline and a strict control over sexuality and desires. This is perhaps made most clear when we look at the widespread suppression of female sexuality and the problem of hysteria dealt with by Freud.

Rousseau's ideas about urbanization and the resultant threats to culture bring us to the third ideal type: control. In focus here is the need to classify and control the growing population. Rousseau's primary concern is about the moral degradation and the threats to individuality that he thinks are a consequence of big city growth. The public space has been filled with threats and dangers. According to Turner, women are hit hardest by these threats, and this results in phobic reactions. This threatening picture allows men to control women and keeps women at home.

And finally, we have Goffman's analyses of how people are increasingly pressured to put their bodies on public display. Among other things, this development is dependent on the absence of stable status markers. Success is more and more a function of the individual's ability to give a correct and winning presentation of himself or herself and his or her body. Today, in order to be a success, one must even look successful – that is, develop a distinct awareness of taste and style. The young, beautiful and hard body has become a sign of happiness and status. This social order leads to contempt for obesity and the occurrence of illnesses such as anorexia and bulimia.

Turner's typology is an attempt to develop a theory of the relation between body, society and illness. Using these four different ideal types, he is also able to capture much of the discussion on modernity, the body and society. Although typologies such as this one have many advantages, I think there are reasons to be critical of attempts to develop a meta-discourse on the social scientific treatment of the body and society.

First, the typology gives us a simplified picture of the relation between psychological disorders and scientific discourses. Should hysteria and anorexia really be interpreted as strategies of resistance? Turner implies as much at the end of his chapter (Turner 1984) when he speaks of illness as a metaphor and as an expression of 'disorder'. It is not entirely clear how Turner views the connection between scientific discourses – Malthus, Weber, Rousseau and Goffman – and mental disorders. We might even question his one-dimensional conception of the actor.

Second, the typology is characterized by only one clear gender dimension, and this bias is never questioned. Turner does mention it in passing, but without any deeper development of questions concerning the relation between society, the body and gender. This missing piece of the puzzle is marked by the absence of any discussion on male psychological symptoms and disorders.

Finally, we might ask ourselves if typologies such as this one are really productive. They can certainly be used to tidy up our thoughts and to develop different categories, but the risk is that in using them we oversimplify and miss those aspects of physicality that are outside the typology's world-view.

Turner's typology is criticized in Arthur Frank's article 'An Analytic Review' (1991). Frank opposes the functionalistic perspective that is the

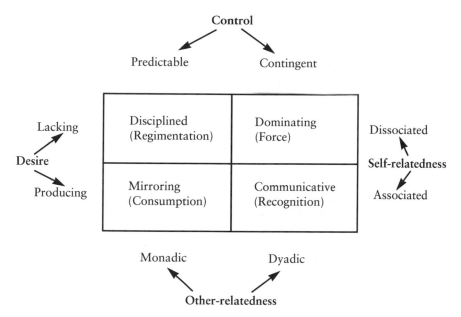

Figure 2 A typology for theories of body and society (from Arthur W. Frank 1991)

point of departure for Turner's typologizing. Instead, Frank wants to start with the perspective of the actor and with a typology that is based on a phenomenological approach. On this point, he is in line with Giddens' thoughts about a structuring process in which actor and structure constitute two sides of the same coin: the ongoing structuring of everyday life and society.

Frank takes his point of departure from four different problems faced by the body: control, desire, the relationship to the other and the relationship to the self. He then constructs a typology and four different 'ideal bodies' (see Figure 2): the disciplined, the mirroring, the dominant and the communicative body.

The *disciplined body* is characterized by great self-control, want, self-sufficiency and a fragmented self. A common theme in Foucault's writings is the disciplined body. This body's contours are shaped via societal disciplinization, but also through self-discipline. Franks stresses the active role of the individual in this process of disciplinization. Even though the purpose of self-discipline is often to reach some kind of goal, paradoxically this strategy often leads to subordination. Thus, this type of resistance commonly results in increased alienation.

The *mirroring body* constitutes a reflection of that which surrounds it, that is, of the consuming society. This body is static and self-sufficient, in that it uses only the world around it to augment its already strong self-image. Desire is allowed to flow freely, but only in order to avoid dealing with underlying deficiencies. This is an aesthetic and narcissistic body that strives to create an integrated experience of wholeness: a mirroring self. This body has perhaps been best described and analysed by Jean Baudrillard.

The *dominant body* is preferably a male body, and has been thoroughly described by Klaus Theweleit in *Male Fantasies* (1995). Here we are provided with an exhaustive description of the construction of the Nazi soldier-man's body and masculinity. What is fundamental to this process is the absence of a basic personality structure. The dominant body is unpredictable. It can exert bloody violence at any point in time. This body is fragmented, but constantly struggling to become whole. A false feeling of coherence and identity is created through the oppression of others and the exertion of violence. But, as already mentioned, this identity is quite fragile.

The *communicative body* is more difficult to pinpoint as an empirical phenomenon. It is characterized by openness to different means of expression and by the will to communicate. Desire is not exploitative, but is instead relationistic and focused on shared enjoyment and sensuality. In this case, Frank turns to dance and other forms of bodily expression. The communicative body is primarily a female body. It should not be thought of as an ideal type, but rather as a Utopian quality. Thus, it is different from the other categories in Frank's typology; in a way, this body is an anomaly.

Although Frank's typology is characterized by a clearer actor perspective and greater dynamics than Turner's corresponding typology, we still have reason to criticize this attempt to frame a discourse on the body and society. Frank's typology is in many ways less deterministic than Turner's, and it also reflects the desire to formulate a Utopia of the body and society. In spite of this, however, I would like to make a few critical remarks.

Even if Frank's intention is to start from the human body and the active actor, in my opinion he tends to have the same problem as Turner in that he objectivizes the actor and the body. The mirroring body is merely an effect of the consuming society and the dominating body is a symptom of specific child-rearing strategies and an authoritarian social system. When we categorize and arrange our picture of reality using typologies, it is often difficult to avoid ending up with a reductionistic model of reality. Even Frank fails to address the question of gender and the body; the male body is dominant, whereas the female body represents Utopian qualities.

Again, the advantage of typologies is that they allow us to develop theoretical categories that can be used to create order in what might otherwise be perceived as a mess. The disadvantage is that we tend to confine ourselves to these categories, thereby missing certain aspects of the reality we want to study. With our point of departure in Frank's categories, we will complete this chapter by discussing various bodies. My purpose is to provide an overview of discussions in which the body is a central theme. If we free these categories from their typological prison and instead use them as starting points for a more unbiased discussion on disciplinization, consumption and power, I think we will find them quite useful.

The disciplined body

At the beginning of *Discipline and Punish*, Foucault describes in considerable detail how Damiens – a poor prisoner who is condemned to death – is tortured and torn apart by four horses. This took place in Paris, on 2 March 1757. It is here that Foucault begins his story of how the external discipline once directed at people's bodies changes, taking on increasingly refined and subtle forms. New and more sophisticated methods of discipline are developed. The brutal external violence against the collective body is replaced by individualized and detailed control of every separate body part. Thus, the growth of new scientific knowledge and the development of new ways to exert power go hand in hand. Foucault writes:

> The historical moment of the disciplines was the moment when an art of the human body was born, which was directed not only at the growth of its skills, nor at the intensification of its subjection, but at the formation of a relation that in the mechanism itself makes it more obedient as it becomes more useful, and conversely. What was then being formed was a policy of coercions that act upon the body, a calculated manipulation of its elements, its gestures, its behaviour. The human body was entering a machinery of power that explores it, breaks it down and rearranges it.
>
> (Foucault 1979: 138)

Using new know-how and techniques, it is possible to exercise meticulous control over people's bodies. Instead of directing this control at the collective, more detailed control begins to be exerted on the individual body. By breaking down the body into its separate parts, new techniques can be developed that lead to maximized utilization of the entire body. Foucault writes: 'The act is broken down into its elements; the position of the body, limbs, articulations is defined; to each movement is assigned a direction, an aptitude, a duration; their order of succession is prescribed' (Foucualt 1979: 152).

Foucault's book about discipline and punishment is an invaluable source for those who are interested in how the image of man-as-machine has imbued various societal practices in different ways. The fundamental idea that knowledge, power and discipline are intimately interwoven is the basis for many investigations of sexual repression, medical care, health care and so on. In Palmblad and Eriksson's study of health information as a mirror of society, *Body and Policy*, we find, for example, the following template that was used in the 1930s to determine children's health status:

> The skin should be moderately moist and have a mild reddish tone. The hair should be soft and shiny, not dry and straggling. The facial expression should be alert and happy, not sad, sallow, dull or listless . . . Good posture is one of the best signs of a well-functioning body . . . The child should have interests, be sociable and show a good ability to cooperate. Relationships to children of the opposite sex should be wholesome.[1]
>
> (Palmblad and Eriksson 1995: 81)

In the three volumes of his series *The History of Sexuality*, Foucault develops his thoughts on the Western outlook on human sexuality. Here, he continues his exploration of the relation between power, knowledge and bodily discipline. When childbirth and family began to be encouraged more and more during the Age of Enlightenment, a war was also waged – under the guise of science – against all forms of sexuality and pleasure that were not suited to this model. New rules were written for the game between power and desire. In terms of sex, Foucault describes four different patterns of power and knowledge. These patterns began to crystallize during the 1700s.

This is, in the first place, a matter of the hysterization of the female body; a process through which it is robbed of its sexuality and made to conform to a patriarchal system of sexual repression. Second, the child's sex is pedagogized and children are defined as pre-sexual beings. This process also leads to a war against masturbation, which is considered to be a sign of illness. Third, childbirth is socialized and subjected to a sweeping process of control. And finally, all forms of 'perverse pleasure' are treated as psychiatric conditions, and ingenious methods are developed for curing people who partake of such forbidden pleasures. The purpose of these patterns of sexuality is to renew, annex, invent and penetrate people's bodies down to the last nook and cranny, and to extend the possibilities of controlling the population.

Foucault's analyses of Western sexuality have greatly influenced studies of the female body and the establishment and maintenance of a patriarchal gender order. However, a common criticism of Foucault is that he tends to analyse resistance and action too little (Giddens 1984, Bartky 1990). Discursive order is focused on at the cost of the active and thinking actor. To be sure, this criticism can be directed at all forms of structuralistic theory, but there is still a point in bringing it up and in looking at the risks involved when we focus unilaterally on the connection between power, knowledge and the body. Therefore, as a contrast to Foucault's work on the disciplinization of the body, we will take a quick look at Frigga Haug's 'memory work', which is described in the book *Female Sexualization* (1992).

In this book, a group of female researchers try to recall early memories of how their bodies have been subjected to disciplinization and sexual repression. Through this memory work – in which memories of how different body parts have been disciplined are brought to the fore – the women attempt to win back their bodies. Women are not viewed as passive victims, but are instead responsible for freeing themselves from the repression that is directed at their sexuality and their bodies. Those women who actively assist in the repression exerted on women in general are called *slave girls*. According to the authors, women have at their disposal a repertoire of different body techniques that are used to hide deficiencies and accentuate positive physical attributes. These techniques are engraved, so to speak, in women's bodies, which makes it difficult for them to free themselves of the limitations inherent in this disciplinization of the body. This knowledge – which is intimately related to self-repression – must be transformed into positive thinking that can in turn be used to free the female body from the boundaries set up by the patriarchal order. In this way, even the flaws in this order can be made apparent.

According to Haug and colleagues, it is necessary to assume that there is an active subject who can recapture her memories and build up strategies in order to liberate her body and sexuality from their bonds to a repressive gender order. By studying the structure of day-to-day life and the micro-power that is directed at the female body on a daily basis, we realize that it is possible to resist this repression. The criticism that is directed at Foucault is similar to that brought up by Giddens. Even if the structuring process includes a close relation between knowledge, power and sexuality, we still have the chance to bring old memories of how our body consciousness has been formed to the fore and, in this way, free ourselves from the limitations in bodily expression that were brought about by this process:

> The extent to which the violence we experience in the process of our development is done to us by ourselves can be shown more clearly by stories of the body than it would be by descriptions of our thoughts, feelings and sensations alone. It is, after all, our bodies that make us unremittingly visible. And it is for this reason that they can be perceived so readily as a reminder of the ever-present need to exert control over the process of our entry into society.
>
> (Haug 1992: 119)

It is interesting to compare Foucault and Haug. Whereas the former exclusively employs discourse analysis, the latter focuses on the life biography and the living person. Foucault's ideas are quite useful for Haug in her search for an analytical model, but she must later develop her own ideas about which strategies can be used in the liberation of the body from its prison. Memory work is an active reflexive process in which the individual, together with others sharing similar memories, can develop new ways of approaching her body. Thus, the disciplined body – both an ideal type and a discursive construction – constitutes the point of departure for reflexive work with the body.

The narcissistic body

The ideal type that Frank calls 'the mirroring body' – or, as I prefer to call it, the narcissistic body – is described as static and self-sufficient. Its basic driving force consists of a desire to establish some form of experiential wholeness – a mirroring self. In this context, Frank joins a sweeping discussion on narcissism, and in my opinion he ends up quite close to Christopher Lasch's conservative and relatively one-dimensional views on this phenomenon. The mirroring or narcissistic body is seen as the product of a mass society, where the media have taken over the rearing of the citizens and where desire has become an end in itself.

This body is perhaps the least successful of Frank's ideal types. The discussion on narcissism is complex and one is easily led hither and thither. Basically, it is about the fundamental preconditions for the formation of a fairly integrated feeling of self. Heinz Kohut, the father of self psychology, has had a great influence on this discussion. According to Kohut, the need for mirroring from parents and the need to mirror these important people oneself are fundamental to the development of the self. When this development is disrupted for some reason, the result is a state of want. This want and the frustration inherent in it lead to the development of narcissistic vulnerability and, with time, even to what is commonly called a narcissistic personality disorder.

Thus, when we talk about narcissism, we are referring to a normal process of development. Everyone needs to be mirrored and recognized. When children are deprived of the basic opportunity to build up a personality and a positive feeling for themselves and their bodies, they often react with aggression and by creating an inner fantasy world to compensate for the absence of an external structure. In this inner world, we find fantasies of omnipotence, aggressive and libidinous instinctual desires and fears of annihilation. In order to understand the complex of problems that is narcissism, we must focus on the relation between these inner fantasies and people's manifest attempts to keep their identities from falling apart.

In modern life, people are subject to frustrations and narcissistic violations. In order to live in modern society, we must attain a balance between our need for security and mirroring, on the one hand, and our search for individuality, on the other. But this balance is only temporary and can even be completely disrupted. When the reflexive construction of the self is threatened, the result can be an individual who experiences deficiency and a fragmentation of the self. The reason a discussion on narcissism is at all interesting today is because many people have perceived and experienced the temporary and unstable nature of the identity. The increased tendency towards narcissistic disruptions in the self-image is the product not only of miserable childhood conditions, but also of a society and a culture in which people are more and more likely to question themselves and their life projects. If this dynamic is to be understood, we must take into consideration its complexity and investigate the positive as well as negative tendencies in late-modern identity formation.

Two things are important here: that we avoid interpreting narcissism in moralizing and negative terms and that we also avoid exalting and applauding it. As I see it, a productive approach involves investigating the psychological, social psychological, cultural and social factors that either facilitate or aggravate the attainment of narcissistic balance (Johansson 1995a,b,c). In the context of discussions on narcissism in the area of culture theory, there has been a tendency to either aim simplistic criticism at the mass or consuming society and to plead for increased moral integration (as Lasch and Frank have done) or to illustrate the positive and radical tendencies of heightened narcissistic sensitivity that characterize modern man (as Marcuse and Ziehe have done). Both of these interpretation strategies are equally one-dimensional (Johansson and Miegel 1995, Johansson 1996a).

Just as Freud once studied the psychopathology of everyday life through slips of the tongue and mistaken actions – thereby showing that all people have neurotic problems – today we can demonstrate that the discussion on narcissism touches on the very foundation of day-to-day identity construction. Those conditions that are called illness or personality disorder are merely extreme variants of 'normality'. The narcissistic body is not only a mirroring body, but a body that actively strives to reach a balance between integration and fragmentation. Similarly, popular culture images and what Frank calls the consuming society are not merely sources of mirroring and passive consumption. These images can also be used to create a subtle and reflexive picture of the self (Fiske 1989). Popular culture can contribute to the development of imaginary identities marked by omnipotence and invulnerability, but it can also help to counteract fragmentation of the identity. Thus, if our examinations on the concept of narcissism are varied and subtle, we can engage in more productive analyses of the effects of popular culture on contemporary culture.

The dominant body

In Theweleit's monumental work *Male Fantasies* we find, for example, the following lines: 'I love unbroken people, men. The kind that are not aware of problems. The kind that stand enclosed in themselves, full of power, calm'[2] (Theweleit 1995: 70). These are the words of Ernst von Salomon, one of the many Fascists who Theweleit allowed to speak. As opposed to the many other authors who have tried to understand and explain Nazism and the men who embodied this Fascist ideology and practice, Theweleit has not used economic, sociological or ideological explanatory models, but has instead concentrated on how a certain type of masculinity is constructed – the soldier-man. In his books from 1977 and 1978, Theweleit anticipates both the discussions on the body and on masculinity that are being carried on by today's social scientists and humanists.

A large part of this extensive work is devoted to analyses of how the soldier-man desperately tries to delimit his body from the surrounding world. Through disgust, contempt and violence, these men struggle to keep their bodies and their identities together. It is the soldier-man's muscular physique and built-up bodily armour that together form the element that must be continuously defended against outside threats. Theweleit writes:

> The muscular physique is identical to his entire self: all control functions, instinct defence functions, everything that determines the soldier-man's conscious thought, what he says, what he writes, his view of himself as a man, his tireless work for the good of the whole – all of this would seem to me to be functions of the body-self, his pain-hardened musculature, that defends itself against fragmentation.[3]
>
> (Theweleit 1995: 662)

Thus, this hard-as-steel bodily armour – the soldier-man's distinctive feature – functions as protection against an underlying want and emptiness.

Women are the greatest threat to the soldier-man's bodily armour. In the first volume of *Male Fantasies*, Theweleit provides a thorough analysis of men's fantasies about the female body. The soldier-man is not satisfied with cleaving the representation of a woman in two – a good part associated with his mother and sister, and an evil part that is projected on to proletarian women and 'whores'. He also empties the good woman of all life and violently destroys the evil woman. According to Theweleit, the soldier-man's primary fear is not that he will be castrated. His fear is much more profound and is directed at experiences of sexuality and lust in general. In one essay from volume I, in which he deals with the notion of flow, Theweleit shows how the soldier-man's ideas about the threat of the red mobs and loose proletarian women are coupled to a more far-reaching fear of what he calls the *flow*. What many authors, for example, Reich and Rolland, describe as desirable – oceanic feelings and experiences of abundant lust pouring over the whole body – is experienced by the soldier-man as a threat to his entire existence. These flows must be stopped at any price: 'not a drop can be allowed to ooze through the bodily covering'[4] (Theweleit 1995: 269).

How are we to understand this? Theweleit dismisses explanatory models in which the blame is put on economic factors or general arguments about irrationality. Instead, he thinks that this is a matter of a specific type of primary and secondary socialization. The soldier-man bodies are impeded early because: '. . . severe hard hands took hold of them and drove the sensations of pleasure out of the skin, through painful corporal punishment, but perhaps also through a temporary or enduring engulfing emotionality on the part of the mother . . .'[5] (Theweleit 1995: 652). This upbringing is then completed through the process of military disciplinization. Theweleit derives the following conclusions from his interpretation of the stories of various soldier-men and from his own research on psychoanalytic theories of development:

> I presume that only very few people in Wilhelmian Germany (and not particularly many more in the rest of Europe) had the good fortune to be fairly finalized at birth. This probably explains why the soldier man's behaviour shows so many connections to that of the normal man. In other words: a fundamentally psychotic type would seem to have been the normal German case. . . .[6]
>
> (Theweleit 1995: 653)

What characterizes the soldier-man's psyche is the fundamental experience of a central situation of discomfort in which he is limitless, undifferentiated and trapped in an all-engulfing symbiosis with his mother. If he is never helped to leave this symbiotic relationship, but is instead marked by obedience, he will defend himself forcefully and with all means against the feelings associated with this basic deficiency. According to Theweleit, this white terror – that is, the violence exerted by these men in order to keep their bodies together – does not have its origins in a joyful acceptance of instincts. This terror originates in these men's attempts to become a self. 'They want to *escape* from their instincts, not give them free rein'[7] (Theweleit 1995: 794, original emphasis). This is not a question of irrational, unconscious elements, but of conscious actions intended to meld together the fragmented ego. Thus, we are not dealing with the classic neurotic, but with the unbounded and fragmented psychotic.

Theweleit's study is impressive in many ways. He points out the central role of the gender dimension in the discussion on power, Nazism and violence. The study even helps us to understand the mechanisms behind many of the gruesome acts committed by the soldier-man. But in spite of this, we still have reason to criticize Theweleit's work. Although he at first takes exception to the one-sided psychologizing of phenomena, this is precisely the approach he ends up taking. For example, we see great similarities on certain points with Alice Miller's studies of Hitler and Nazism. Theweleit compares classic Freudian psychoanalysis to the ideas of analysts such as Mahler, Balint and Klein. What he seeks is the very foundation of the body perception and construction of masculinity that characterize the soldier-man. However, there is a danger inherent in broad generalizations and psychologizations such as those used by Theweleit, in which the body of the soldier-man is synonymous with almost all masculinity. The dominant male body thus becomes a symbol for a society and system of upbringing that have failed. According to Theweleit, we should not consider the sort of man that was the subject of his investigation to be separate from men in general. His subjects are only the tip of the iceberg of patriarchy. Here we find no alternative male identities or bodies. The process of social disciplinization has led to nearly complete subordination.

Theweleit's analyses seem relevant as long as he limits himself to guerrilla soldiers and those men who were among the core of the Nazi troops. However, this approach renders alternative male bodies and identities impossible. With this study, Theweleit joins the feminist criticism of the 1970s, which was directed at all types of masculinity. Today, the complexity of the construction of gender has been recognized both within feminism and within the growing field of men's studies. In his book *Masculinities*, Connell tries to develop a theory of the relation between different types of masculinity (Connell 1995).

Connell differentiates between *hegemonic, complicit, subordinate* and *marginalized* masculinity. *Hegemonic masculinity* – characterized by the strong, solitary and hard man – stands for the defence of a patriarchal order in which men are superordinate and women are subordinate. This type of masculinity is embodied by men in the military, politics and other positions of power. But, according to Connell, most men do not satisfy this definition of masculinity. On the other hand, there are many men who, in various ways, are *complicit* in the maintenance of the gender order, but these are more communicative and democratic men; men who do not beat women and who try to establish a relationship of equality with their partners. *Subordinate* masculinity has the lowest rank on the male power hierarchy. These men are usually perceived as feminized and non-masculine. The concept of *marginalized* masculinity is used to discuss power relationships between men – relationships based on class and ethnicity.

This picture is complicated further when we begin to discuss the relation between hegemonic, complicit, subordinate and marginalized masculinity. Thus, if we are to understand the construction of contemporary gender identities, we must study the relation between different types of masculinity and different types of femininity. Given this, Theweleit's analyses of the soldier-man should be seen as a study of the development of one specific masculinity and body. What remains is an exploration of the relation between the soldier-man's body and masculine identity, on the one hand, and other types of masculine identities, on the other.

The communicative body – an anomaly

When Frank talks about the communicative body, we leave the world of ideal types and enter the realm of Utopias. What characterizes this body is primarily its activeness, creativity and communicativeness. Frank writes:

The body continues to be formed among institutions and discourses, but these are now media for its expression. For the communicative body institutions and discourses now enable more than they constrain, while in the other body styles the opposite balance prevailed.

(Frank 1991: 80)

The communicative body is a good body. According to Frank, it is preferable that this is a female body. He illustrates his thinking with a discussion on dance. Here he means that there is sometimes a potential for liberation and creativity. The expressive and communicative body is one possibility, but its expression is often threatened by the social disciplinization of bodies. By describing the communicative body as a Utopian aspiration, Frank relegates all sorts of actions, reflexivity and change to one 'wastebasket' category in his typology of the body and society. Thus, what does not fit into the stable categories he has built becomes a type of anomaly.

In studying Turner and Frank's typologies, we are made aware of the limits inherent in this way of working. As soon as it becomes interesting to discuss actors and processes of change, we inevitably end up outside the typologies. The structuring process that Giddens describes in *The Constitution of Society* always contains a relation between power and resistance (Giddens 1984). Structuring the identity and the body is an ongoing process; structures are never entirely limited, but are also made possible. The actor always has a choice, even if this choice is more or less restricted.

In this survey of several different theories of the body and society, I have tried to show how it is possible to study the relation between hegemony and various forms of resistance. None of the bodies discussed by Turner and Frank is unambiguously disciplined, dominant or narcissistic. We can possibly use these ideal types in order to clarify certain mechanisms and discursive strategies, but it is always necessary to continue the discussion and to study in detail the concrete structuring process that is taking place in day-to-day life. If we break these different 'bodies' away from Turner and Frank's typologies, and instead use their typifications as a starting point for discussing the effects of the process of societal disciplinization, we can develop a more varied and subtle analysis of the relation between the body and the culture. In my rather sketchy attempts at such an analysis, I have tried to point out a few navigable roads. A theoretical development of this kind is in great need of deliberations on subjectivity and the inner psychological world.

The body and the sociological imagination

The purpose of this presentation has been to discuss the productive aspects of the discourse on body and culture that has emerged in Great Britain,

France and elsewhere. By beginning with several well-known typologies, my intention was to show the weaknesses inherent in those theories of the body that focus exclusively on the process of disciplinization *per se*. If we, instead, take our point of departure from Giddens' idea that agent, structure and system constitute a whole and develop in relation to one another, we can avoid making deterministic analyses of the body and culture. Even if societal disciplinization does encroach on everyday life and form people, there are always at least a few degrees of freedom within which individuals can act and form their own bodies.

The reason for bringing the body into social psychology is that introducing this notion focuses the spotlight on real, living people and how they experience our time. The one-dimensional person exists only in our analyses of society and the individual; reality is much more complex. People's bodily experiences are an important aspect of the structuring of day-to-day life. We experience the world through our bodies; words and sentences are our attempts to capture and represent these experiences. Even if we do not always succeed, we still express this ambition in our language games and in the discourses that sociologists then spend their time analysing. I am promoting a social psychology of the body, and I think we should open our sociological imagination to those aspects of reality that are experienced and structured via physical sensations.

Notes

1 Translated by K.W.
2 Translated by K.W.
3 Translated by K.W.
4 Translated by K.W.
5 Translated by K.W.
6 Translated by K.W.
7 Translated by K.W.

8 Mediazation, identity and multiculturalism

Dreamtime and everyday life

Mediazation and the everyday

Nowadays, much of people's time is spent using some form of media. For many people, the media structure the day's shape as well as its content. By switching between different media and making a selection of programmes and activities, it is, in effect, possible to live in a media world, completely cut off from social 'reality'. We often hear horror stories about computer nerds who sit glued to their computers, elderly people whose entire view of reality is derived from the media and young people who become extremely violent and act out what they have seen in violent films. Some postmodern theoreticians even claim that we live in a totally simulated 'reality', and that it is no longer possible to distinguish between what we experience through the media and social reality.

Although I am not willing to go so far as to talk about a completely mediatized and simulated day-to-day life, it is clear that the growth of the media has changed the conditions for identity formation in our late-modern culture. In this chapter, I will distinguish between three different ways in which mediazation has influenced the shape and content of everyday life: the privatization of the public, the breakdown of social and cultural distinctions, and the creation of information gaps. Only a short discussion of these three processes will be provided. Whereas these changes primarily have far-reaching consequences for the social and cultural structuring processes affecting people's media use, we can also discern different individual and collective approaches to media choice. In the following presentation, I will discuss two types of consequences of the mediazation of everyday life: those causing the dissolution of social and cultural distinctions and those causing increased differentiation.

The privatization of the public

In our day and age, the boundaries between the private and the public have gradually shifted and, in some cases, have even disappeared. The media have played a clear and important role in these processes of change. In his now classic study on the electronic media's effects on human behaviour, Joshua Meyrowitz claims that the media have helped to blur the boundaries between the back regions – that is the private regions where people reveal their feelings, problems and desires – and the front regions, where more well-controlled behaviour is often displayed (Meyrowitz 1985). Many of the expressions of emotion that were earlier shown only in the back regions and in the private and intimate sphere are now exposed publicly, sometimes without people's consent. The photographic media relentlessly uncover details of the most intimate sort – pictures that are able to reveal the very things people most want to keep secret. Facial expressions, slips of the tongue, clothing, body language and so on lay bare intimate details of a person's emotional response patterns and his or her ability or inability to maintain an adequate public presentation of the ego.

According to some researchers, the media have taken over the function of the church as a channel for various types of confessions. Through the media, we can take part in both private and political confessions. The private is made public and the public is privatized. In talk shows (confession programmes) such as, for example, *The Oprah Winfrey Show* and *Ricki Lake*, people's private lives are exposed in an often bizarre manner. Although the intention of such programmes is to provide intimate and revealing pictures of people's private problems and emotional lives, there is considerable evidence that these pictures are often the result of more or less well-directed performances. In a study on this type of programme, Laura Grindstaff describes how the selection of programme guests was carried out in one case:

> When *Diana* producers did a show about acquaintance rape, they debated back and forth about who to lead with: the woman repeatedly raped, stabbed, and left for dead, or the woman raped once by her best friend. Ultimately they decided to go with the second woman because she was a better storyteller, even though the story itself was less harrowing. Sometimes producers will switch guests at the last minute depending on what transpires in the Green Room. If guest no. 3 proves more excitable and easier to fluff, producers may bump guest no. 1 and put no. 3 in her place.
>
> (Grindstaff 1997: 182)

The more aware people become of the importance of presenting themselves in a pleasing and winning way, the more time and energy they spend on their style, language, clothes and so on. In a study on contemporary media, John Thompson describes how soldiers on patrol in politically sensitive areas are often extremely conscious of media coverage (Thompson 1995). This awareness can lead to the staging of certain events and the concealment of others. Politicians are similarly subject to constant observation by the eyes of the media. Mistakes made while under surveillance can have disastrous consequences for political careers. Thompson describes how US president Gerald Ford committed a *faux pas* during a campaign:

> President Ford displayed his unfamiliarity with Mexican food when, on a campaign rally in San Antonio, Texas, he was served hot tamales by his hosts. As television cameras focused on his mouth, he proceeded to bite into the tamale; but the symbolic act of consumption was immediately aborted because he had failed to remove the corn husk in which the tamale was wrapped.
>
> (Thompson 1995: 142)

Meyrowitz discusses how feelings, mistakes and awkwardness literally 'ooze' out of the television screen. While watching TV, we are taking part in an ongoing construction of social reality. The distinctions between private and public, and between individual and collective, are no longer tied to physical space, but are instead retrieved at a discursive level, where they are shaped and take the form of a symbolic struggle between different perspectives (Hartley 1992). The emotionology developing in the wake of mediazation can be described as an exceedingly delicate mixture of increased intimatization and heightened self-control. People who are constantly subjected to media scrutiny must develop secret-keeping strategies, or otherwise risk being engulfed by the media public's simulated world.

In accordance with Benjamin's descriptions of the media, people have – through the images they are constantly bombarded with – become quite observant and aware of details and subtleties they never would have noticed had their attention not been drawn to them. Popular culture also supplies a rich assortment of images that focus on and produce style, body ideals, emotional expression and so on. This has led to increased reflexivity and alertness to the risks of being cited incorrectly or presented in a negative light in the discursive world of the media.

Intermediary regions and the imaginary transgression

The electronic media have not only affected the distinction between the private and the public, they have also contributed to the dissolution of central social distinctions. For example, women now have access to a man's world that was earlier closed to many of them. According to Meyrowitz, this creates *intermediary regions* where we find combinations of male and female features and where opportunities for the illusory crossing of social barriers are formed (Ewen 1988). Such intermediary regions make creative encounters, *bricolage* and carnivalesque experiences possible.

In the past, when authorities were created, kept in power and protected by the 'secret society', the conditions were right for kindling respect for the patriarchy and the powers that be. Today, however, authority is constantly being scrutinized. And even though all-out criticism is rarely aimed at the entire power structure, cracks in the foundation are uncovered continuously. Meyrowitz writes about how this crisis of legitimacy is partly created through the influence of the media:

> There is an inherent 'vanishing truth' paradox in the use of television to give us a close-up view of our politicians, experts, doctors, psychologists, teachers, and other authorities. When we see our leaders in varieties of situations and locations, when we observe them as they respond to spontaneous interviews as they grow weary from a day of work or campaign, we do not simply learn more about them. By searching behind the front of performers, we also change the roles that can be performed and perceived – as well as the images that high status performers have of themselves.
>
> (Meyrowitz 1985: 168)

When the boundaries between the worlds of men and women, adults and children, and authorities and citizens are partly nullified in the media, the prerequisites for change are also created. Such a dissolution of boundaries can be thought of as something positive, but also as a dangerous tendency in our time. What is positive are our increased chances to question unnecessary polarizations and strategies of super- and subordination. The negative consequences lie, for example, in children and young people's increased familiarity with violence and the exploitation of sexuality.

Of course, this imaginary transgression of economic, status and social barriers does not automatically result in real change. But just as, for example, Radway and – following in her footsteps – Giddens have shown, such illusory processes can lead to changes in how we view love relationships and this, by extension, can lead to real social change.

Information gaps

If Georg Simmel were alive today, he would certainly be horrified at the continuously growing amount of information now circulating on the global market. Simmel did not see any natural connection between the growth of the culture and people's acquisition of knowledge and wisdom. Although he tended to develop an overly dismal and simplistic view of 'the culture', many of today's information-optimists would benefit from a confrontation with

Simmel's more sceptical attitudes towards cultural development. The things we call 'information' and 'culture' do not automatically lead to human development and improved life conditions.

The mass media are always utilized in a particular social and cultural context. In part, this implies differentiation in terms of which types of media are used, which contents are consumed and which consequences this media use has for the individual's chances of realizing his or her life plans. The value of individuals' cultural capital is not determined by the number of computers, TV channels or video machines they have, but by how these resources are used. Some authors also differentiate between low and high information capital. If information is to affect the individual's social position in any real or significant way, it must be transformed into social resources. For those individuals who have already learned the right cultural codes and who understand the rules of the societal distribution-of-power game, media use can play an important role in the acquisition of additional power and status.

In societies where day-to-day life is largely permeated and structured by media use, it is possible to see a number of different media strategies. Certain social groups have succeeded in acquiring considerable cultural capital and also in converting this capital into economic and material advantages. In such cases, weekend movie-going and buying a new CD constitute part of the particular cultural taste that is well suited and complementary to certain types of professional ambitions and pretensions of status. Whereas this type of media use is quite strategic and reflexive, other media patterns that result in fewer economic and cultural advantages in the social power arena can, of course, also be discerned. Clearly, just as there are social differences in a nation, there are also interindividual differences in media use and its consequences.

Globalization and the propagation of certain types of culture have long been an integrated aspect of modernity. Although it is impossible to distinguish certain unequivocal consequences of the globalization of the media, it is clearly the case that Western ideals and power claims tend to catch on on a global basis. The Western media hegemony reigning in the world today has a number of ideological and material consequences. But for people in other parts of the world, Western media can sometimes have paradoxical consequences. We will return to these soon.

There is no simple, unambiguous relation between the media world's imaginary images and the shaping and content of everyday life. More and more, however, day-to-day life is being structured and filled with meaning through the media. And it is here that we find the great differences between how various social groups and different individuals choose to shape and to allow themselves to be influenced by their media use. The way in which we choose to let the media structure our everyday lives and fill them with certain forms of symbolic material is of decisive importance for how we position ourselves in the social power arena. And although there is an element of freedom in this choice, it is largely prestructured and dependent on factors such as class, status, gender and ethnicity.

Mediazation, power and paradoxes

The mediazation of society has a number of disparate consequences for people's identity formation. This development can lead to the solidification of already existing power hierarchies or to the creation of new ones. Also, the imaginary transgression of such super- and subordinating structures can lead to reflection and sometimes even to real social change. The media are not outside the power arenas within which the distribution of various types of societal resources is determined. Thus, the consequences of mediazation are certainly not unambiguous, but instead are dependent on the symbolic struggle over who will define social reality and how we should understand our place in that reality.

In the above, we have concentrated on certain structural changes in social reality. But mediazation also has more specific consequences for how people choose to interpret and understand their lives and for how they choose to act given these different understandings. Through an introduction of Stuart Hall's ideas on how the reception of media messages varies, we will now try to formulate a few thoughts on how media reception is expressed in late-modern society.

What is hegemony?

If we are to begin to understand how people use and are affected by the media, we must first discuss how power is reproduced through the mediazation of society. Certain perspectives and points of view will always have a greater influence on how the important political and social questions are formulated and responded to. And encoding as well as decoding of media messages always takes place in the context of certain specific societal power configurations. In his influential article 'Encoding, Decoding', Hall set the agenda for how these types of discussions on power have been formulated since the 1970s (Hall [1973] 1980).

Hall's point of departure is the notion that there exists in society some form of dominant cultural order. This cultural hegemony is tied to the cultural, political and economic powers in society in different ways. Hegemony is in no way static and unchangeable. The ways of thinking that are dominant at a given point in time are constantly subject to critical examination and are drawn into the power struggles occurring between different classes and status groups in society. Hall's definition of a hegemonic point of view is the following:

The definition of a 'hegemonic' viewpoint is (a) that it defines within its terms the mental horizon, the universe of possible meanings of a whole society or culture; and (b) that it carries with it the stamp of legitimacy – it appears coterminous with what is 'natural', 'inevitable', 'taken for granted' about the social order.

(Hall [1973] 1980: 17)

Hall distinguishes between four different codes that are used during the interpretation of media content: *dominant/hegemonic, professional, negotiated* and *oppositional*. In theory, the dominant code implies reception characterized by total and uncritical acceptance of the dominant viewpoints reproduced in the media. The professional code represents the partial reinterpretations that are made by journalists and others working in the media, often within the framework of the hegemonic code. The negotiated code is described as follows:

Decoding within the *negotiated version* contains a mixture of adaptive and oppositional elements: it acknowledges the legitimacy of the hegemonic definitions to make the grand significations, while, at a more restricted, situational level, it makes ground-rules, it operates with 'exceptions' to the rule. It accords the privileged position to the dominant definition of events, whilst reserving the right to make a more negotiated application to 'local conditions', to its own more *corporate* positions. The negotiated version is thus shot through with contradictions, though these are only on certain occasions brought to full visibility.

(Hall [1973] 1980: 18, emphasis in original)

Finally, we have the oppositional code. This reading often involves criticism of the hegemonic point of view and a complete reinterpretation of it in favour of an entirely different perspective. The point of departure for such a standpoint is often strong political consciousness and a critical approach to the ruling political system.

Hall's analysis of the hegemonic structure of the media and his distinctions between different types of decodings constitute a fruitful starting point for a discussion on media and power. While this work does provide us with a broad framework for our analyses of media use, we must, of course, fill in many details. His encoding/decoding article brings up a number of problematic questions: how are we to understand the relation between specific power structures in society and the media's reproduction of a given content? How is a certain hegemony created and to what extent can it be said to permeate everything from soap operas to news programmes? What different types of negotiated decodings can possibly be discerned? And so on.

In the following section, I will discuss different types of negotiated codes and relate them to Hall's definition. Moreover, I will attempt to deal with the difference between cases in which the dominant ideology is clearly expressed in the media and cases comprising often more diffuse, ambiguous and problematic encodings.

Reflexivity, irony and ambivalence

Within the scope of power

When Hall developed his model of the process of encoding and decoding during the 1970s, reception research was not as sophisticated as it is today. Much of the media research developed in cultural studies has shown how people actively use the media in their identity work. Thus, it is difficult today to construe any sort of antagonism or even a clear distinction between media use and identity development. It is instead the case that the growth of a familiarity, with and relation to, the media is an integrated part of contemporary identity formation. Media use is a natural and perhaps even central aspect of the reflexive identity project (Thompson 1995).

With no pretensions to covering the topic completely, I will now provide several examples of how people develop different approaches to the media and to popular culture. I assume, as does Hall, that the decoding of media content always takes place within the scope of society's hegemonic order, but I will also emphasize how the negotiated 'reading' of media content is often accompanied by an active use of this content in our identity work. While media use leads to the development of *individuality*, a *dependence* on the media and popular culture is simultaneously created. A negotiated reading can, thus, result in the undermining of society's hegemonic order, but in the long term, this reading can also contribute to the strengthening of the hegemony. What distinguishes the negotiated code is a certain degree of confusion and obscurity in terms of the outlook on power and the media. I will first focus on the relation between reflexivity and irony, and will touch on how contextual factors affect the decoding of media contents. This will be followed by a discussion on the oppositional approach.

Reflexivity and the strategies of the popular culture

Whereas a great deal of early media research dealt with how people are affected by their own consumption – that is, the *effects* this activity had on their actions – and how they develop a false and uncritical consciousness, the aim of present-day research is to understand how people integrate and use the media in order to form their identities. This transition from describing relatively passive consumers to describing actively engaged consumers has also brought with it a reconceptualization of the relation between reception and media choice. What we see is a clear individualization in terms of where, when and how people use the media. In combination, increased knowledge about how the media work and increased access to a more and more differentiated media selection make active identity work possible.

This increase in the reflexive use of the media is made clearer when we study how young people approach and consume the various mass media products. Looking back to the beginning of the 1900s, we see that, in Sweden, young people's consumption of, for example, detective stories and American films was cause for a near moral panic. Representatives for society's educated classes were extremely negative towards young people's – especially working-class young people's – consumption of 'trash culture'. At the beginning of the twentieth century, sales of Nick Carter's book were successfully blocked and constant attempts were made to censure American films. During the 1960s and 1970s, the youth culture was cause for more or less continuous eruptions of moral panic. But the result of these moralists' attempts to counteract the harmful effects of the popular culture and to put a stop to various phenomena in youth culture was often that precisely these phenomena were reinforced and attracted more and more young people to subcultural activities. Today, we can even observe that the creation of moral panics has become part and parcel of the marketing of popular culture.

In her study of the rave culture, Sarah Thornton has shown how the 'devils' created through moral panic are often perceived as heroes in various subcultures and youth cultures. It is even the case that new and greater interest in aspects of the youth culture is created through misinterpretations of, and morally agitated reactions to, just these phenomena. Thornton writes: 'What could be a better badge of rebellion? Mass Media misunderstanding is often a goal, not just an effect, of youth's cultural pursuits. As a result "moral panic" has become a routine way of marketing popular music to youth' (Thornton 1995: 120).

With time, young people belonging to a specific subculture have learned to use the media to increase the cult value of their own culture. Thornton also states that overly positive coverage and attempts to transform subcultures into mainstream phenomena are often these cultures' kiss of death. In 1988, acid house was portrayed as a pleasant phenomenon of youth culture by the tabloid newspaper the *Sun*. The paper contained numerous tips on the types of style marker that could be used to slip into this subculture. Thornton writes:

Had the tabloid continued with this happy endorsement of acid house, it is likely the scene would have been aborted and a movement would not have ensued. Similarly, rave culture would probably have lost its force with this second wave of positive reports had it not been followed by further disapproving coverage (about ravers converging on free festivals with 'travellers', namely, nomadic 'hippies' and 'crusties' who travel around the countryside in convoys of 'vehicles').

(Thornton 1995: 136)

The reflexive use of the media also creates a gradual dependence on these media. Drawing a sharp dividing line between everyday life and media use is becoming increasingly difficult, if not impossible. The media have a strong influence on how we structure our day-to-day lives and they also help to fill life with content and meaning. People's memories are filled with the content of popular culture, affective states are coupled to specific forms of media use, and the lifestyles and youth cultures we see today are permeated by distinct patterns from the popular culture. In the rave culture – and many other subcultures – we find an ambition to criticize the dominant, mainstream culture and to provide an alternative to it. However, this reflexive and deliberate approach can easily become an ironic strategy in which media use constitutes part of a lifestyle based on the avoidance of being deadlocked and unequivocally defined.

The ironic generation

In Douglas Coupland's first novel *Generation X. Tales for an Accelerating Future*, published in 1991, we meet a gang of youngsters whose lives revolve largely around their media experiences. Their life happenings and desires are tied to the media or to the fashion industry in various ways. Andy, Claire and Dag are in their twenties, well educated, unemployed, fanatically independent and pathologically ambivalent. They experiment with different lifestyles and 'Mcjobs' – low-paid and temporary work – and try to live in what Baudrillard would certainly have described as an 'aesthetic hallucination of reality'. Generation X actually consists of a countless number of subgroups. One of these is called the 'Basement subculture':

> Basement subculture was strictly codified: wardrobes consisted primarily of tie-dyed and faded T-shirts bearing images of Schopenhauer or Ethel and Julius Rosenberg, all accessorized with Rasta doohickeys and badges. The girls all seemed to be ferocious dykey redheads, and the boys were untanned and sullen. No one ever seemed to have sex, saving their intensity instead for discussions of social work and generating the best idea for the most obscure and politically correct travel destination (the Nama-Valley in Namibia – but *only* to see the daisies). Movies were black and white and frequently Brazilian.
>
> (Coupland 1991: 26, original emphasis)

The intensive job of seeking an identity and lifestyle sometimes leads to blind alleys and feelings of non-identity. The type of identity embodied by the three young people in *Generation X* is not primarily coupled to the individuals' life histories and their relationships to family and friends, but instead to a world populated by media personalities and consecrated objects. This is a brittle and frail identity – one that is always changing. Although we are given momentary glimpses of seriousness and existential anxiety, these characters' identity work is largely characterized by ironic distance, an inability to get involved and the will to believe in some project completely. The feeling of being a fraud – someone who never takes life seriously – eventually takes root among Coupland's young characters:

> But basically, my life-style escape wasn't working. I was only using the *real* Basement People to my own ends – no different than the way design people exploit artists for new design riffs. I was an imposter, and in the end my situation got so bad that I finally had my Mid-twenties Breakdown. That's when things got pharmaceutical, when they hit *bottom*, and when all voices of comfort began to fail.
>
> (Coupland 1991: 27, original emphasis)

In this book, media use is not part of the characters' ambition to formulate a specific identity or group affiliation. The youngsters Coupland describes are instead marked by the same spirit of the times and by the fact that they are always on their way somewhere else. These young people are able to elude the confines of a well-defined identity by recklessly exploiting the media and popular culture. Instead, their identity consists in the fact that they move freely in a mediatized world and that they consistently reject all hegemonic demands. This, in turn, generates existential anxiety, and feelings of rootlessness and identity confusion are developed.

Polysemy and social differences

What characterizes much of popular culture is its openness to a number of different interpretations. This creates the conditions for various types of identity work. Naturally, media use can be understood in terms of the factors dealt with above – that is, affiliation with different subcultures or belonging to a specific generation. But much of the use of popular culture can be tied to more basic social distinctions. For example, John Fiske has shown how people express a certain resistance to the hegemonic order through their interpretation. This resistance need not, however, be the expression of a deeply considered political ideology and it certainly need not result in action.

Depictions of violence are often popular because they thematize super- and subordination and because they make the illusory transgression of society's hegemonic order possible. In his book *Understanding Popular Culture*, Fiske writes about how people in certain parts of Latin America tend to interpret the portrayals of Hispanics in *Miami Vice* as positive. He writes:

> A colleague returning from Latin America reported to me that *Miami Vice* was popular there because of its portrayal of Hispanics (albeit as villains) with all the trappings of success in a white society: the popular

pleasure in the drug baron's displays of mansions, speedboats, limou-
sines, servants, women, and swimming pools far overrode their narra-
tive defeat by Crocket and Tubbs – indeed, their ultimate defeat by the
forces of order is necessary for the construction of relevance.

(Fiske 1989: 136)

Such illusory attacks on the hegemonic order do not constitute active
attempts to defeat it, but they can be interpreted as expressions of discon-
tent with the way things are. Fiske also describes how 'subordinated' men
enjoy seeing, for example, Rambo and Rocky films. In these films, the hero
always succeeds in re-establishing the subordinated man's masculine
honour. According to Fiske, media use is an important element of the social
psychology of subordination. By seeing certain films, playing certain computer games and questioning 'good taste', members of the lower class are
able to protest against the unfair social circumstances that contribute to
their destitution.

As long as the protests are not clearly formulated – but instead constitute
spontaneous emotional reactions – they will not result in the development
of alternative Utopias or in dreams of a better life. In contrast to the
emotional discharges Fiske describes in many of his analyses of popular
culture, Hall's oppositional strategy represents a will to change society; a
consistent reinterpretation of the hegemonic order in favour of some type
of radical change. In the next section, I will provide a few examples of how
this can be manifested.

Power and resistance

One cornerstone in Meyrowitz's analyses of how the media structure social
reality relates to the media's ability to break down existing social distinctions. This can be manifested in different ways. Earlier in the book, I have
touched on several of the consequences of this process of historical change.
In addition to affecting the distinctions between male and female, child and
adult and so on, we can also imagine that the media have the power to
produce global effects. In his book *China Turned On*, James Lull describes
the growth of a critical Chinese public that has been influenced by and used
media material in order to formulate its criticism of the ruling political
system. The loosening of regulations and the partial abolishment of censor-
ship during the 1980s have created the conditions for a reflexive process.

The media that once spread the dominant ideology of the state and portrayed the ideal worker, have changed and moved towards a more Western
model. The Chinese can now watch the international news via satellite, thus
taking imaginary trips to foreign countries. These types of vicarious experience and the broadening of the sphere of experience contributed to an
increasingly critical approach to the dominating order in China. Lull writes

that: 'Lightning fast and ultimately uncontrollable television has instead given rise to a diversity of cultural and political sentiments in China at a speed that disrupts stability and control' (Lull 1991: 209).

The reception of soap operas and other types of popular culture content created a potential for the growth of a critical public. Among other things, Lull describes the enormous success of a soap opera that was aired as a 12-part series in 1986, which was about the power struggle between a young, beautiful political reformer and a rigid, traditional bureaucrat. This soap opera thematized the conflict between old and new that threatened to demolish the existing political system – a conflict that also led to the tragic events in China in 1989.

The more obscure the societal hegemony becomes, the more difficult it is to formulate an oppositional position. The functioning of this code is at its best when it is possible to identify clear power constellations and to formulate an oppositional standpoint towards a cultural hegemony that is anchored in, and spread through, these constellations. It is more difficult to identify a clear hegemony in a society where an enormous selection of TV channels, films, videos, radio stations and so on is offered. Different angles on social problems and societal development are often available. But sometimes clear discursive formulations of a hegemonic nature occur as well.

In his book *The Persian Gulf War* (1992), Douglas Kellner shows how the US media 'swallowed' the government's official policy towards Iraq and Saddam Hussein without reservation. Through a combination of gross simplifications, misinformation and a consistent message that Saddam Hussein was unwilling to compromise, support for the government's war policy was drummed up. All attempts on Iraq's side to come to a peaceful solution or to negotiate were quickly rejected as unreasonable. The media were agents for a relatively rapid escalation of an atmosphere of war. Kellner illustrates how the large groups of media companies – which also have great interest in the war industry – and politicians from both parties were united in their effort to escalate the conflict and to take up arms. Kellner's argument is that the media's consistent creation of images of an insane ruler and a fanatical, war-hungry people played an active role in generating the preconditions for an armed conflict. By systematically conjuring images of a reactionary, fundamentalist people and by stressing the impossibility of unarmed communication, other types of solution to the conflict were successfully counteracted. The result was the sweeping destruction of Iraqi resources and people and the reinforcement of the image of the USA as the global police.

However, when all is said and done, the situation described by Kellner – in which a country's media, politicians and other power centres are united by a single hegemonic viewpoint – is uncommon. But there are also more basic cultural formations that, in spite of the fact that they are changing, show relatively great consistency over time. This is the case, for example, for representations of masculinity and femininity or ethnic/national affiliation.

In the following section, I will deal with the media's engagement in today's discussions on the multicultural, diverse society.

Multiculturalism as market merchandise

In late-modern society, social and cultural differences constitute both a basis for discrimination and a celebration of cultural diversity. When we talk about *cultural* differences, we are often referring to differences related to ethnicity or nationality. But cultural differences are equally a matter of class or gender, and it is often difficult to differentiate a particular difference when factors such as class, gender and ethnicity form complex and interwoven patterns. As mentioned, however, when we talk about the multicultural society, we are usually referring to ethnic differences. Roughly speaking, we can distinguish between two types of discussion on cultural diversity. On one side of the coin, we have questions concerning the problems of integration and segregation in society. On the other side, we find tributes to multiculturalism as a source of change and regeneration.

The media, of course, engage in this discussion in several different ways. Television programmes, films and other forms of media presentation that reinforce existing conventions and misrepresentations of Asians, Blacks and other ethnic groups are continuously reproduced. Although such media presentations of ethnicity are not always as clear as they might be and are sometimes even conveyed quite subtly, they help to strengthen the feelings of alienation many ethnic groups feel – alienation from Western culture and from their own position in this culture. In her books, bell hooks has shown how Western dominance is reflected in various films and representations and how the result of this is the marginalization of, for example, Blacks (hooks 1992). In a similar manner, Said (1978) examined the Orientalism that in many ways permeates Western perceptions of Islam, Muslims and 'The Orient'.

However, the media do not only convey openly racist and prejudiced representations of the other. They also reproduce a more subtle exoticism in which 'otherness' is presented as something desirable. This exoticism can, of course, be expressed in many different ways (see Sernhede 1997). In a book on the global music industry, Taylor writes about how so-called world music often tends to exploit various types of ethnicity. He writes: 'Authenticity is jettisoned and hybridity is celebrated, but it is always "natives" whose music is called a hybridity' (Taylor 1997: 12). Of course, questions of what actually constitutes a culture or how the celebration of different 'ethnic traits' should be viewed are quite sensitive. Historically, exoticism has had the effect of accentuating certain features at the cost of others: Blacks have been viewed as sensual, sexually overactive and musical; Asians as wise and so on. But exoticism such as this naturally leads to the fortification of an already existing super- and subordination.

Thus, ethnicity becomes exotic and sought after, and can thereby be sold and consumed in the form of images and representations of the unknown. bell hooks writes: 'Within commodity culture, ethnicity become spice, seasoning that can liven up the dull dish that is mainstream white culture' (hooks 1992: 21). What would seem to be positive images can, thus, additionally reinforce ethnic stereotypes and add to oppression. hooks relates overhearing a conversation between a few of her male students. They talked about the great opportunities there were for experiencing 'ethnic sex', that is for going in for sexual relations with Black women, Asian women and so on. Images spread through the media encourage such oral and consumption-oriented approaches to the opposite sex.

There are, of course, also a number of representations that modulate and call into question stereotypes and ethnic biases. However, the risk is that these will drown in the flood of Orientalism and other types of stereotyping that flourish in, for example, action films and thrillers. Thus, in spite of the levels of awareness associated with ethnic discrimination, the media continue to contribute to the solidification of certain attitudes in their audience – an audience that is prepared to 'consume' the other.

Mediazation and identity

The mediazation of everyday life has a number of consequences for how we approach and discuss questions of identity development in late-modern society. Roughly speaking, we can distinguish three different consequences of mediazation: the structuring of day-to-day life, the calling into question of social distinctions and of hegemonic demands. Paradoxically, this development leads both to increased chances for questioning the dominant social order and, in some respects, to the reinforcement of this order.

The structuring of everyday life occurs largely with regard to mass media use. Today, individuals have every opportunity to design a pattern of media use that fits the lifestyle they have developed. The increased selection of different media and the possibilities for combining them allow for great individualization of media use. At the same time, more and more identity spaces are created and we see an increased dependence on the media. A structure is developed in day-to-day life that revolves around certain television programmes, series, computer games or whatever else is of interest to people and shapes their lives.

Because it is possible to study other people's experiences and 'worlds', there is also more room for the illusory transgression of boundaries. Meyrowitz points out how the media have helped to pull down different cultural barriers. This change need not, of course, result in real change, but there is always the possibility that it will. Perhaps it is the case that the media give people's dreams and desires the nourishment that is necessary for them to initiate action and change. The transformations pointed out by Meyrowitz have changed the prerequisites for modern-day identity formation. But if we are to address how these structuring processes affect people's perceptions and actions, we must also take into account the reception process *per se*.

Written in the 1970s, Hall's encoding/decoding model is a simple mental diagram that still works as a point of departure for discussions on, and analyses of, the media's influence on human thinking and behaviour. Even if the processes described by Meyrowitz have resulted in the general calling into question of many social distinctions, it is, in the end, a matter of how individuals choose to approach a given text and how they assimilate and interpret various representations and images. We still, in many respects, think and act within the confines of certain dominant conceptions about how society should be organized, about the relationships between different social groups, about specific configurations of power and so on. At the same time, doubt is constantly being cast upon these configurations, and the struggle over how we should create a good society is ongoing.

People's stories about themselves and the reflexive formation of an identity take place more and more within the framework of a mediatized society and everyday life. The media do not merely fill these stories with content, they even help to structure people's existence. To a greater degree than in the past, contemporary biographies and novels are filled with references to popular culture and to the mediatized reality. Today, in order to talk about identity at all, we must be able to come closer to, and understand, people's great involvement in the popular culture. In the modern world of fiction, we meet individuals who are obsessed with, and quite knowledgeable about, popular culture. To understand these characters, it is necessary to master the art of intertextuality and to have the same know-how. For example, how – without this know-how – are we to understand Nick Hornby's character when he compares his new love to Susan Dey: 'Marie is pretty, in a cross-eyed American sort of way – she looks like a plumper version of Susan Dey, after *The Partridge Family* but before *L.A. Law* – if you're going to launch into a spontaneous and meaningless love affair you could do much worse' (Hornby 1995: 57).

9 The global gym: masculinity and femininity in the age of deception

The global body

Recently, strong criticism has been aimed at the cult of beauty and the narrow aesthetic body ideals that are propagated in the media and in advertisements. Feminist researchers have pointed out that this cult and the worship of the beautiful and perfect body have caused more and more women to develop various types of eating disorders (Bartky 1990, Bordo 1990, Craik 1994). According to these researchers, the beautiful and perfect bodies we are constantly bombarded with through magazines, advertising, films, TV and so on shape our ideals and create restricted normative ideas about our bodies. The mass media have also helped to spread Western conceptions and beauty ideals at the global level. How this has affected and will affect cultural variation in beauty ideals is a question that has largely been left unaddressed.

If mediazation can be blamed for the spread of Western beauty ideals, then the gym culture must be held responsible for manufacturing the bodies that circulate through the various mass media. The people we see in US films and TV series do not have 'natural bodies'.[1] Their bodies have been formed and produced to suit a specific ideal that is deeply rooted in Western culture. Today, although we can create an attractive image using make-up, clothes, touch-ups and other techniques, it is necessary to develop a basic shape that matches the aesthetic ideals dominating the media industry. The gym provides the requisite body techniques for creating the 'perfect body'. These techniques are always being refined and improved so that we can develop increasingly finished and ideal bodies.

Although interest in body-building has a long history, it was in the 1970s that this body technique and life philosophy were first distributed on the global market. The International Federation of Body-building was formed by Joe and Ben Weider in the USA and Canada in 1947 (Gaines and Butler 1977, Dutton 1995). Toward the end of the 1970s, the federation had more than 100 member countries and the number of individual members was increasing. The internationalization of body-building also laid the ground-work for a billion-dollar industry and for the global circulation of equip-ment, classes, instructors and a life philosophy; a specific attitude towards life and physical training that is cultivated in this body culture. Body-build-ing has more recently become a public sport and it continues to spread throughout the world, though under the heading 'fitness'. The concept of fitness implies a broadening of a body culture that has its roots in more classic forms of body-building. In addition to fitness and strength training, fitness also includes the range of body techniques called aerobics. It is increasingly common for people to combine strength training with some type of aerobics in order to attain maximal training results.[2]

Using gym-made bodies in films and on TV is not a new phenomenon. In 1930, the following item about Greta Garbo was printed in the Swedish periodical SWING: 'Over there, sloppy training certainly will not do. Ask Greta Garbo! She was forced to complete a several-month-long course in special *Physical Culture* and the results were so good that she has never since neglected her daily dose of fitness' (SWING 1930,11: 13). If we look at the pictures of actors from the 1930s and well into the 1970s, we see that rather full and 'soft' female bodies are common. But the 1980s and 1990s have witnessed gradually increasing demands that film actors and photographers' models should have perfect bodies.[3] What counts today is hard bodies. The connection between the gym culture and the film industry has grown stronger. It is not unusual for the film star of today to have started their career as a model. And superstars who want to retain their status are forced to spend considerable time in physical training and body care.

The global body culture not only influences people's perceptions of their physical beings, but also their gender identities and, thereby, their sexuality. Both female and male bodies are construed as objects of desire – as alluring images of sensuality, sexuality and lust. Although it is primarily female bodies that have been circulated on the global market, today we see a rising interest in aestheticizing the male body. When we study contemporary images of men and women, we can see both a tendency towards less clear distinctions between the sexes and a return to polarized gender roles. In this chapter, I will take a closer look at how these different tendencies are affected by the global gym culture. This culture not only influences our body ideals, but also our notions of masculine versus feminine.

When I talk about the *global body*, I am referring to a tendency towards the idealization of a specific physical form – the hard, well-trained body –

that has become more and more prominent in the media and advertising. This ideal has an increasingly greater impact on everyday life through the media and the fitness industry. Even though the gym culture has not caused the development of this body cult, it has certainly helped to kindle these tendencies and has created the conditions for a hitherto unseen interest in the perfect body. Today, we have every reason to talk about the *global gym*. By this I am referring to the international circulation of goods and services intended to propagate the gym culture. What the exact effects of this development will be on our outlook on masculinity and femininity is still uncertain. The gym culture's influence on people's perception of gender is not unambiguous. This culture would seem to take hold in the paradoxical situation prevailing today; a situation in which the masculine and the feminine constitute the very centre of people's perception of reality, while the function of these categories as markers for clearly delimited identities has deteriorated.

I will begin by exploring several tendencies in the development of Western body ideals. This discussion is based on research on the modern history of the gym culture. Moreover, I will argue that the hard body has become established as an ideal and a norm. This body will serve as a bastion against, and a counterweight to, the ambivalence that characterizes contemporary people's lifestyle. The hard body becomes a normative ideal for both men and women, and this has a number of consequences for the formation of gender. Next, I will develop several thoughts on the paradoxes that mark today's Western outlook on sexuality and gender. The title of this chapter refers to the strong influences that media images have on our perception of masculinity and femininity. I will conclude by discussing the question of how much stress should be placed on the effects of mediazation on people's day-to-day life and awareness.[4]

I want to emphasize that we are dealing with modern-day tendencies. Just as there is a cult surrounding the hard, well-trained body, there is also a tendency towards just the opposite. High-life disorders, poor fitness and obesity are problems that are regularly raised by physicians and other healthcare workers. However, I choose to focus on the former tendency, well aware of the paradoxical circumstances that prevail in the contemporary culture.

The perfect body

Although there has been great historical variation in beauty ideals and views of the body – especially when we compare different cultures – there seems to be a certain continuity in Western notions of what constitutes a beautiful and perfect body. In *The Perfectible Body*, Kenneth R. Dutton traces two different male body ideals and their development, from the sculptures of antiquity to the modern-day gym and the sculpted bodies created there.[5] On the one hand, he observes the warrior body; the heroic, powerful and muscular man. This body is created for the heat of battle and symbolizes power and dominance.[6] On the other hand, we have the erotic-sensual male body. This body is less muscular than the heroic one, but is supple, hard, slightly muscular and radiates sexuality and sensualism. Both of these bodies reoccur as a main thread throughout Western history. In some cases, the heroic body dominates and, in others, the erotic-sensual body is more influential. Whereas the heroic male body constitutes a hegemonic ideal image of masculinity, the other type can be seen to represent the promise of a more sensitive masculinity.

In warring cultures, it is the heroic body that dominates, whereas the feminized male body is given more room in times of peace and consumption. This is made quite clear in the consuming culture – especially during the 1970s – where the mediazation of everyday life promotes the growth of more androgynous ideal bodies.[7] However, in the 1980s and 1990s, we see a tendency towards a renewed worship of the hard, heroic body. Both men and women are attracted to the hard body, and in contrast to the androgynous ideal of the 1970s – which signalled a revolt against all superfluous distinctions and a celebration of the transgression of borders – the androgynous ideal of the 1990s is an expression of both men's and women's yearning for stability, identity and boundaries. Paradoxically enough, the body ideals of both of these periods have the same effect – they lead to the dissolution of the distinction between masculine and feminine. During the 1970s, men were to get in touch with their feminine side and recognize the erotic-sensual body. In the 1990s, women are approaching their male side – building muscles, hard bodies and becoming masculinized.

Body-building is often associated with heroic male super-bodies. This was especially clear during the beginning of the twentieth century. The body culture that developed in Scandinavia during the 1920s and 1930s had strong ties to the growth of nationalism. The male body would come to symbolize an aggressive form of nationalism, with clear inclinations towards xenophobia and racism.[8] The body should be hardened and 'cleansed'. An entire life philosophy based on the heroic male body was developed in body-building instruction books written during this period; this system of thought also included a strong negative attitude towards 'the feminine'.[9]

During the post-war period, the US film industry was growing and, with this, the male body-builder body was given new significance. Although the muscle-men were often cast in heroic roles, their half-naked bodies received longing looks from women as well as men (Wernick 1991, Cohan and Hark 1993, Neale 1993). The film industry created a more ambivalent and contradictory picture of the male body-builder body. In a way, the male body was feminized and made into an erotic object. Even if we try to separate the image of erotic-sensual masculinity from the image of heroic masculinity, they come together more and more. Although there is certainly a clear demarcation between the male pin-up and the body-builder, both of these types of male bodies are included in a process of change in which the aestheticized male body is given increasing amounts of public space.

During the 1990s, the hard, fresh, well-trained, fit body symbolized success and happiness. Nowadays, the body techniques and life philosophy that originally developed within body-builder circles are spreading to a wider and wider group of people who are interested in their own bodies. The hard exterior is primarily an expression of a disciplined approach to the body and of aspirations for success and the good life. But this hard exterior also sends out signals of restrained sensualism and withheld longing for bodily pleasure. The hard male and female body of the 1990s is an exceedingly paradoxical phenomenon. The archetypal masculinity that is represented by the warrior body and the grotesque body-builder body has fallen by the wayside and been replaced by a body that constitutes a combination of sensualism and masculine hardness. The male and female body approach one another again, but now as the result of a common worship of the hard, well-trained body.

The philosophy of the hard body

The hard, muscular body has been a male ideal since antiquity. As mentioned, the aggressive-dominating body side of this ideal has been emphasized during certain historical periods, whereas during other times, this side of the philosophy of the hard body has been toned down while the erotic-sensual male body has been accentuated. During the past few years, we can see how these ideals have been united more and more in the so-called fitness body. This also implies a shift from a purely masculine warrior body to an androgynous fitness body.

The warrior body fills all of the personality-type criteria we usually attach to a dominant and hegemonic masculinity: aggressiveness, callousness, goal orientation, uncompromisingness and disdain for weakness. This male body can be likened to a machine that reaches its goals without hesitation. Such masculinity has been depicted in, for example, Klaus Theweleit's classic study of the German soldier-man in the 1930s (Theweleit 1995). These men have contempt for all forms of weakness and their body armour serves as a defence against both internal and external threats. Their fragile identities are threatened by everything that is vague and indefinable. They strike out mercilessly against that which threatens to awaken their deep feelings of ambivalence and uncertainty towards life. Thus, their masculinity rests on an extremely weak foundation and can easily turn into an aggressive struggle for power. These men anchor their life philosophy in their hard bodies – a life philosophy intended to create a strong race that can help to build and defend the nation.

We meet a similar type of hard body in many Hollywood films produced during the Reagan years. In her study, Susan Jeffords shows how the male heroes depicted in films such as *First Blood* (1982), *Die Hard* (1988), *Lethal Weapon* (1987), *Robocop* (1987) and so on embody an aggressive, dominating type of masculinity that is well suited to Ronald Reagan's conservative politics (Jeffords 1994). These film heroes strive to re-establish a patriarchal masculinity. They use their strong, hard bodies in order to fight the bad guys who threaten the vision of a society ruled by an omnipotent father figure: a patriarch who has no tolerance for threats to his authority. This type of hard body bears witness to a masculinity that ruthlessly fights and destroys its enemies and that safeguards the family and the nation. In other words, this is not a communicative and sensitive masculinity, but instead an action-oriented and uncompromising masculinity that is held up as an ideal for the heroes of the Reagan era.

The hard body is clearly delimited from the surrounding world. This body's exterior signals unambiguousness and clarity. There is no room here for ambivalence and contradiction. Everything that threatens this unity is combated using all means. But the body that has developed within the framework of the contemporary gym culture is somewhat different from the hard, heroic male body described and analysed by Theweleit and Jeffords. Like the soldier-man or Rambo, the representatives of the gym culture seek unambiguousness and clarity, but they are not as successful in their struggle against ambivalence.[10] At the gym we find different variations on the hard body: everything from enormous, heroic bodies to slim and trim model bodies. But most bodies are a combination of the erotic-sensual body and the heroic body.

At a concrete and obvious level, the hard, gym-made body constitutes an attempt to develop an absolutely healthy lifestyle. The weaknesses and disadvantages associated with this project are illustrated by, for example, unhealthy states of dependency, drug abuse and a sometimes badly concealed contempt for people who do not celebrate the hard body. This bewildering combination of health and ill-health characterizes many contemporary phenomena. The struggle against ambivalence and the search for order often seem to result in the opposite, that is the absence of structure and order.

In today's gym culture, all forms of fat are a threat to the perfect body. The build-up of fatty tissue is counteracted by a combination of body techniques: physical training, diet, plastic surgery and a well-thought-out lifestyle. Flabby, boundless fat constitutes a threat to aesthetic and beauty-fixated physicality.[11] Although the hard body can be thought to represent aspirations for order and structure in life, the body culture – paradoxically enough – helps to make the drawing of boundaries between masculine and feminine, asceticism and hedonism, freedom and dependency, health and illness, and so on, more problematic.

The gym is often considered to be the place where we cultivate archetypal male and female ideals. And even if this is partly correct, there would also seem to be other tendencies at work in today's gym culture. The relation between the varying and static features of this culture is always being shifted, and many symbolic battles are fought over how the masculine versus the feminine should be defined and delimited. This is especially clear with regard to the phenomenon of female body-builders, a subject to which I will return later.

During a time of constant crises, in which everything that is permanent is evaporating, the gym is naturally an alluring place for many young people. Here, they are able to create some form of security – a stable identity and habitat. Such efforts to anchor identity claims spatially are characteristic of late-modern man (Johansson and Miegel 1995, Johansson 1996c). Today, however, more and more people have also realized that this is a hopeless enterprise. We must learn to live with the contradictions and the lack of truths and everlasting values that have been so well explored by post-modernity (Johansson 1998). If the gym is also shown to be a sphere of ambivalence and the hard body is revealed to be the superficial, empty shell and the mask it actually is – what happens then? Can the gym accommodate a diverse group of people and life philosophies or will it, instead, foster intolerant and body-fixated young people?

Aesthetics, sexuality and gender

Gym-made bodies have long been objects of desire for both women and men. Within today's gym culture, the hard, beautiful body is idolized as both an aesthetic and a sexual object. The body that is sculpted to perfection is revered partly because it symbolizes success and hard work, and partly because it awakens sexual urges and desire. It is simultaneously an extremely gender-neutral creation and a sexualized and gender-definite one.

It has become increasingly common for men and women to train at the same gym, on the same premises. Among young women, the interest in strength training and muscles has increased markedly. On the other hand, a similar tendency on the part of men – an increased interest in aerobics – cannot be observed. Although it is still the case that women largely cultivate slender, thin and fragile bodies, they are showing up more and more at strength training gyms. Their initial motives are to develop a more well-defined body – a body with clearer contours – but perhaps also later to build up muscles and a more solid body. Today, we see increasing numbers of young women with muscular and 'defined' bodies. Most men at the gym are not trying to develop a grotesquely large, body-builder body, but are content with becoming muscular, supple and well trained. Even though both ends of the continuum can be seen at the gym – bulky, massive male bodies and thin, fragile female bodies – we can also see a tendency towards the convergence of masculinity and femininity. A hard, slightly muscular, dynamic and supple body has become the target for both men and women. Every detail of this physique is attended to with the greatest of care.

At the gym and, thereby, also in the mass media, the minimalistic aesthetics of narcissism is being cultivated more and more. This aesthetic is not primarily aimed at the whole or at a total experience of people as body and spirit, but instead at the inherent logic and mystery of different body parts.[12] Body-builders can spend considerable time in front of the mirror looking at a single body part – for example, biceps or shoulders – completely fascinated by how that part of their body increasingly emulates the ideal created in the gym culture. Individual body parts are charged with narcissistic energy and elevated to the status of cult objects. Schwarzenegger's arm is worth its weight in gold, as are Pamela Anderson's silicone-filled breasts and Demi Moore's bottom. In the pictures circulated in body-building and fitness magazines, it is not the body in its entirety that is depicted; instead various body parts are focused on and shown in all their glory.

The body techniques developed in this culture are also aimed at training each body part until the limits of perfection are reached. Similar to the statues of antiquity and other prototypes of current body ideals, the contemporary gym-made body is a sculpted body. Meticulous work and considerable time have been devoted to forming the body into a perfect representation of the mental images found in Plato's world of ideals. But as long as we are unable to fully live up to these ideals, we are eternally doomed to pursue the image of the perfect body, the perfect partner and the perfect life. Our longing for the good life has perhaps never before in history been expressed in forms such as those marking the contemporary body culture.

It is seldom, however, that this longing for the good life goes deeper than the aesthetic surface to which so much trouble and energy are devoted in the gym culture. Enormous sums of money and much hard work are invested in perfecting the exterior; in creating a hard body, shaving off unsightly hair, taking care of everything that leads to disorder. Beauty blotches are attended to through training, diet and plastic surgery. Men and women are united in their struggle to create an ascetic and aestheticized body. But while they are united in this cult of physicality, they are also careful to maintain the distinction between the sexes.

The politics of minimalistic narcissism are intended to recognize similarities, as long as it is possible to construe and establish some kind of boundary between the sexes. Men and women are united in the cult of the youthful, perfect body. This hard, almost genderless and aestheticized body is raised to the level of a superordinate ideal, and the mass media force people to relate to this ideal in one way or another. This does not, however, imply that this androgynous ideal has resulted in a total dissolution of people's ambition to maintain a gender order and polar identities. Although men and women are reflected in the same ideal mirror image – that of the hard body – the identification cannot be driven to the extent that it threatens the gender order and our understanding of the basic differences between masculine and feminine.

Even if the masculine and the feminine seem to be approximating one another at the gym, the minimal distinctions are still safeguarded. The boundary between the sexes is maintained via gender markers in the form of partial objects: breast, penis, rear-end and mons pubis, and through clothes and make-up that emphasize body parts differently for men as opposed to women. When these distinctions are called into question or threatened, strong emotional reactions can be triggered. The female body-builder is the embodiment of doubt about gender distinctions. Through her powerful, muscular body, she is able to bring the question of the biological versus cultural nature of gender to a head (Johansson 1995b). For many, a defined and reduced female body-builder body is an extremely male phenomenon. Within body-building circles, fierce debates about the phenomenon of female body-building have occurred. According to many, it goes against nature, whereas others have asserted women's right to train their bodies and compete on the same terms as men. The women who are active in this branch of sport are not interested in being viewed as masculine, but are instead careful to bring out their femininity. When hard physical training and the continuing battle against fat result in reduction of breast tissue, it is not uncommon for women to seek out plastic surgery in order to retain their female shape.

But while those within the body-building culture and fitness movement try to avoid threatening people's need for normality and order at all costs, this culture constantly reproduces anomalies and, thereby, helps to raise doubts about the gender order. Not only is the boundary between masculinity and femininity challenged by an androgynous body ideal that has more and more advocates, but the half-naked, hard body is also being sexualized and made into an icon. Within, for example, gay culture, the undressed male body that adopts various poses and that is depicted in photographs and in films has had considerable attraction value. Although few body-builders have openly declared their homosexuality, there is a large group of homosexual men who are interested in this sport and the homoerotic qualities that can be read into the pictures circulating on this body market.[13]

Despite attempts to desexualize the body-builder body, it is difficult to avoid the sexual connotations and cravings that are the product of a culture that celebrates the naked, perfect body. It is primarily contextual factors that distinguish the body-builder body from the male stripper body; the stripper comes in close contact with his customers, whereas the male body-builder poses on a stage and has a certain distance from his audience. The minimalistic narcissism that thrives within the gym culture contributes to the sexualization of various body parts. On the meat market of partial objects, people no longer seek the entire body, but instead get lost in the beauty of the parts. Perhaps the absolutely perfect body can only be formed using parts from different human bodies. Can we imagine a kind of cyber-inspired Frankenstein whose component parts were chosen with more care than in the original story – a creature that can only be made in a simulated world where perfect combinations of perfect body parts are possible?[14]

The global gym

In the late-modern global society, the demand for beautiful, perfect bodies has been continuously on the rise. Such bodies command a high price on the international market. Photographers' models and actors can make fortunes on their appearance and their aura. This cult surrounding the beautiful body is nothing new. But modern science has made possible a closer examination of the human body and the development of techniques that can be used to create a perfect physique. Gradually, and without our reflecting on it, the norms for what should be aesthetically attractive have become increasingly narrow and out of reach. One can no longer be born with an ideal body; it must be formed through training, diet and surgery.

The bodies we encounter on the TV screen or advertising signs are not 'natural'. These bodies are specially designed to appeal to people and to be admired for their godlike quality. Physical figures such as these would be impossible without the techniques of the gym culture. Miracles can certainly be made with plastic surgery, but the full creation of a perfect body also requires good underlying material. Thus, success also requires a willingness to sacrifice leisure time, friends and a normal life. An inevitable requirement is the willingness to devote large amounts of time to working on the body at the gym.

The gym is the factory where the 'global body' is displayed and refined to perfection. Before this type of body has reached its audience, it has often gone through additional aesthetization and treatment so that it can fulfil the requirements of the ideal body. Thus, those bodies that are circulated and sold on the global market are the ultimate proof of 'the body as construction' (Butler 1990, 1993). Although those in the gym branch usually point out that certain genetic conditions are necessary to create a beautiful body, they also emphasize the unlimited possibilities that we have today to form an ideal physique through training, diet and lifestyle. Advertisements for various training techniques and diet preparations must be interpreted as strong arguments for the total plasticity and formability of the body. But nobody has claimed that success is a question of luck. It can be achieved only through hard work and an extremely ascetic lifestyle. Thus, in order to enjoy and reap all the profits they can from their bodies, individuals must give up many of the 'good things in life' and be willing to devote practically all of their time to training and body care.

The global body is still a polarized creation; a male and a female body. But while people continue to admire the hard male warrior body and the slender female Barbie model, a more androgynous ideal is also being formed. This time, however, it is not a matter of recognizing 'the feminine', as it was during the hippie period when young men and women let down their hair, celebrated love and dedicated themselves to life's pleasures. Now it is a question of an androgyny that is centred around the hard body. The ascetically afflicted body is melded with the aestheticized-erotic body and, thus, an ideal is formed to which both men and women can pay tribute. Even if this androgyny implies a convergence between masculinity and femininity, the gender distinction is still maintained using minimalistic criteria.

People no longer talk about the body as a whole – for example, the motherly, plump body versus the muscular male body – but they are instead increasingly fixated on those body parts – the individual units – that can be used to distinguish one person from another in a definite manner. Ideally, the hard body is appended with either extra-large breasts or a pair of gigantic biceps. The more impossible it becomes to distinguish male and female culture or to define gender as two separate worlds in other ways, the more development there is of minimalistic criteria that can serve as guarantors of the gender order. Thus, while we can observe a rise in the androgynization of bodies, we can also see a polarization of masculinity and femininity.

The global gym has contributed to the polarization of gender, but it has simultaneously created the conditions for a specific body ideal – the hard body – that is embraced by men as well as women. Thus, this body – a result of modern body techniques – creates the conditions for the development of an androgynous body ideal. This ideal is then distributed over most of the world through the mass media and advertisements. The perfect body lacks individuality; it exists on the plane of ideas and is an abstraction. The bodies and faces we often encounter in the mass media are deceptive in the sense that they are created in order to pay tribute to the idea of the perfect body.[15] These bodies are created through intensive training and modern media techniques – retouching and other methods of editing the picture material. At best, they are furnished with some kind of individuality, in this way becoming a little more human. A unique face or some type of 'beauty flaw' can create an individual distinctive character.

The global gym also has its backbiters, many of whom object to the fitness prophets' message of health, training and a 'sound' lifestyle. There are other ways to live the good life. But, at the same time, it is difficult to avoid being confronted with the bodies that appear on the TV screen, in advertisements and various magazines. For many people, these bodies function as a bad conscience – a reminder that they eat too much, exercise too little and, most importantly, that they don't look like the people who populate the media world. Such a bad conscience can be transformed into internal torment that drives people to a life of constant dieting, deprivation and despair. It is young people who are primarily affected by this cult of beauty and the body. But in this way, more people are reminded of the transience of life and of the impossibility of trying to live up to the ideals that prevail in today's culture. If the global fitness culture is a threat to people's individuality and psychological well-being, then it is also a threat to the good life. The question is whether we can learn from the gym culture's accumulated knowledge on health and training and use it to promote a healthy way of life, without being drawn into the extreme cult of the hard body.

Notes

1 This is meant as a criticism of the idea that natural bodies exist at all.

2 The latest phenomenon, at least in Sweden, is the so-called *life circuit*. This is a computer-based training programme led by personal trainers which includes different types of body techniques.

3 Body stars such as Arnold Schwarzenegger and Jane Fonda have made significant contributions to this development. See, for example, Schwarzenegger and Hall (1974), Fonda (1981), Fonda and McCarthy (1984), Green (1988) and Anderson (1990).

4 The body of research on gyms, fitness and body-building is extensive. See, for example, Green (1986), Klein (1990, 1993a,b), Fussel (1991), Mansfield and McGuinn (1993), Johansson (1995a, 1996b and 1998), Aoki (1996) and Lloyd (1996).

5 Dutton's book is a rich source of reflections on the historical development of different body ideals. His main focus is on the male body.

6 This hegemonic male ideal has been discussed by Georg Mosse (1996).

7 For a discussion on the consuming culture and the body, see Featherstone (1991a,b and 1994).

8 This is clearly illustrated in body-building instruction books written at the time (see, for example, Berg and Windmarken 1933).

9 In my book *The Sculptured Body* (1998; in Swedish: *Den skulpterade kroppen*), I develop my thoughts about these questions more thoroughly. For a more extensive discussion on the hard, warrior body, I suggest reading Theweleit's study of the physicality of the soldier-man (Theweleit 1995).

10 See Bauman (1990) for a discussion on modernity and ambivalence. We can, of course, discuss the extent to which Jeffords' hypothetical male strategies can be thought of as 'successful' and if they actually were able to counteract ambivalence.

11 Threats to societal order in the form of dirt and other types of disorder have been thoroughly treated in Mary Douglas' classic study (1970).

12 For a thorough discussion of narcissism and culture, see Johansson (1995a,c, 1996c). As opposed to the aesthetics of narcissism, which is a question of worship of the entire body as form and surface, the minimalist aesthetics of narcissism is the cult of what in psychoanalytic theory are called partial objects, that

is, individual body parts: a fixation on, and desire for, perfect biceps, breasts, bottoms, calves and so on.

13 Dutton (1995) discusses these questions in detail.

14 Haraway (1990) has introduced the notion of the cyborg as the ultimate sign of the plasticity of the human body. Although this encounter between perfect simulated bodies is, so far, only found in the popular culture – for example, the simulated sexual intercourse in *Lawnmower Man* or the brutal sex murders in *Strange Days* – it is not inconceivable that the pornography industry of the future will take advantage of these ideas and techniques.

15 My reasoning here is partially inspired by Hartley (1992).

10 Conclusions: social psychology in the twenty-first century

A social psychologist is a person who finds himself or herself constantly struggling with the issue of how we should approach and conceptualize the question of the relation between the individual and society, or, if you prefer, between actor and structure. He or she is not interested in finding a definite solution to the problem of making this relation seem straightforward and understandable. Such a 'solution' would mean the death of social psychology and, thereby, high unemployment among social psychologists. What fascinates the social psychologist – and helps to make working in the area an exciting and whodunit-like activity – is partly the fact that the task they have taken upon themselves cannot be completed.

When we talk about the relation between the individual and society, we are operating in a borderland. When the English psychoanalyst D.W. Winnicott uses the term 'transitional area', he is referring to the psychological region that develops *between* the mother and the child. This region is characterized by an indefiniteness and by an uncertainty with regard to what actually arises from the mother as opposed to the child. This is the region of fantasy and creativity. The objects and ideas that are created within the framework of this region are never definitive or 'objective'. The transitional area is the abode for both play and creativity. The strength of social psychology is that it helps to establish such an area and to give us the opportunity to reflect on how human identities are formed in a relatively complicated society. Through his positive outlook on the meta-theoretical imagination and by generating new concepts and ideas, the social psychologist can help to bring to the fore the dynamic that marks different social and cultural processes.

One of the most important tasks of the social and cultural sciences is to stimulate new ways in which we can look at our culture and the world around us – that is, to stimulate a perspectivist vision. The social psychologist's job is to constantly counteract the trivialization that threatens much of the work in the social and cultural sciences. This is why these theoreticians have, in general, little respect for many of the strict rules for how science should be done – rules that characterize the work of many contemporary social and cultural scientists. Social psychologists get their inspiration from various disciplines, cross boundaries and question established 'truths', and do not hesitate for a second before enriching their work with literature, poetry, film and art. But this does not mean that the social psychologist has given up all ambitions of doing science. Instead, they want to contribute to a change in how we view science.

While today's social psychology is losing certain of its traditional features and characteristics, new opportunities for doing this kind of work are also being created. However, the outlook on social psychology presented here should not be misinterpreted and used as a justification for calling just about anything social psychology. Instead, I would like to claim that heavy demands are placed on people who want to be called social psychologists. Such people should be able to move between different disciplines and possess a broad and deep knowledge of society and culture. They should be interested in theoretical speculations as well as empirical studies. It is only through the combination of these two interests that social psychologists can test the validity of the different concepts they have developed.

In this book, I have presented a number of different theoretical perspectives. Among these it is possible to include a number of theoreticians and 'schools'. As mentioned at the outset, my purpose has not been to introduce all types of contemporary social psychology. Selections were guided by my personal preferences and by my attempt to reconstruct a social psychological 'tradition' with deep roots in early sociology. Part II was intended to bring to life some of the theories and perspectives presented in the theoretical part of the book. Towards the end, we gradually approached a contemporary discussion on the individual and society/culture.

I have avoided incorporating, for example, cultural studies, feminism and postcolonial theory into the theoretical chapters for various reasons. In the first place, doing these areas justice would have required an additional 100 pages. Second, describing this contemporary theoretical diversity and the changes it will surely imply for the social psychology of the future would require a separate book. And this would require a thorough consideration of the relation between contemporary philosophy of language and social psychology. Much of contemporary theory development is marked by the radical questioning of earlier ways of conceptualizing and discussing the actor and the subject, and integrating this into social psychological thinking would require an exhaustive treatment.

If we compare the social psychology that developed at the beginning of the twentieth century with the social psychology taking form today, we can see that today's version presents us with a considerably more complicated picture of the individual as well as of society and culture. In other words, our chances of doing interesting and exciting social psychological research today are great. In spite of this, however, researchers continue to produce studies that are inspired by a meagre meta-theory and that lack an adequate treatment of the relation between the individual and society.

This is why we still need social psychology; not as a separate discipline, but as a meta-theoretical field. Among other things, the task of social psychology should be to inspire us to reflect on the formation of contemporary identities, to serve as a seismograph that is sensitive to new societal tendencies and to document changes in the interplay between the individual and society. When we try to turn social psychology into some kind of technical or objective knowledge-base, we also spoil our chances of critically reflecting on and developing a creative approach to our ongoing observations of social reality. Just as Winnicott's transitional areas constitute a prerequisite for human creativity, social psychology constitutes an opportunity for social and cultural scientists to take a creative approach to their work as researchers and analysts of contemporary life. The field of social psychology nourishes and adds a splash of colour to research that is intended to say something about our age. Thus, even in the future, it is doubtful that we can do without social psychology.

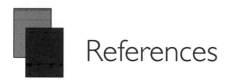

References

Adorno, T., Frenkel-Brunswick, E., Levinson, D.J. and Nevitt Sanford, R. (1950) *The Authoritarian Personality*. New York: Harp Brothers.

Alvesson, M. (1989) *Sociala störningar av självet*. Lund: Studentlitteratur.

Anderson, C. (1990) *Citizen Jane. The True Story of Jane Fonda*. London: Virgin Press.

Anderson, N. ([1923] 1967) *The Hobo*. Chicago: Chicago University Press.

Andreas-Salomé, L. ([1921] 1962) The dual orientation of narcissism, *Psychoanalytic Quarterly*, 31: 1–30.

Andreas-Salomé, L. (1964) *The Freud Journal of Lou Andreas-Salomé*. London: Quartet Books.

Andreas-Salomé, L. (1972) *S. Freud and Lou Andreas-Salomé, Letters*. London: The Hogarth Press.

Aoki, D. (1996) Sex and muscle. The female bodybuilder meets Lacan, *Body & Society*, 4: 59–74.

Asplund, J. (1983) *Tid, rum, individ, kollektiv*. Stockholm: Liber förlag.

Auster, P. (1985) *The New York Trilogy*. Harmondsworth: Penguin.

Bartky, S-L. (1990) *Femininity and Domination. Studies in the Phenomenology of Oppression*. London: Routledge.

Bauman, Z. (1990) *Modernity and Ambivalence*. Oxford: Polity.

Bauman, Z. (1993) *Postmodern Ethics*. Oxford: Blackwell.

Bauman, Z. (1995) *Life in Fragments. Essays in Postmodern Morality*. Oxford: Blackwell.

Bauman, Z. (1997) *Postmodernity and its Discontents*. Cambridge: Polity.

Beck, U. ([1986] 1992) *Risk Society*. London: Sage.

Beck, U. ([1993] 1996) *Att uppfinna det politiska*. Göteborg: Daidalos.

Benjamin, W. (1950) *Berliner Kindheit um neunzehnhundert*. Frankfurt am Main: Suhrkamp Verlag.

Benjamin, W. (1992) *Paris 1800-talets huvudstad. Passagearbetena*. Stehag/Stockholm: Symposion.

Berg, E. and Windmarken, S. (1933) *Muskelbyggaren. En bok om fysisk träning*. Göteborg: Laurins.

Berger, P., Berger, B. and Kellner, H. (1973) *The Homeless Mind: Modernization and Consciousness*. New York: Vintage Books.

Berman, M. (1987) *All that is Solid Melts into Air*. New York: Simon & Schuster.

Blumer, H. (1937) *Symbolic Interactionism: Perspective and Method*. Englewood Cliffs, NJ: Prentice-Hall.

Blumer, H. (1954) What is wrong with social theory? *American Sociological Review*, 19: 17–25.

Blumer, H. (1969) *Symbolic Interactionism: Perspectives and Method*. Englewood Cliffs, NJ: Prentice-Hall.

Bordo, S. (1990) Reading the slender body, in M. Jacobus, E. Fox Keller and S. Shuttleworth (eds) *Body/Politics: Women and the Discourse of Science*. New York: Routledge.

Bourdieu, P. (1984) *Distinction: A Social Critique of the Judgement of Taste*. London: Routledge & Kegan Paul.

Buck-Morss, S. (1993) *The Dialectics of Seeing. Walter Benjamin and the Arcades Project*. Cambridge, MA: MIT.

Bulmer, M. (1984) *The Chicago School of Sociology. Institutionalization, Diversity, and the Rise of Sociological Research*. Chicago: University of Chicago Press.

Butler, J. (1990) *Gender Trouble. Feminism and the Subversion of Identity*. London: Routledge.

Butler, J. (1993) *Bodies that Matter. On the Discursive Limits of 'Sex'*. London: Routledge.

Camus, A. ([1942] 1993) *Främlingen*. Stockholm: Albert Bonniers.

Cohan, S. and Hark, I.R. (eds) (1993) *Screening the Male: Exploring Masculinities in Hollywood Cinema*. London: Routledge.

Connell, R.W. (1995) *Masculinities*. Cambridge: Polity.

Coupland, D. (1991) *Generation X. Tales for an Accelerating Future*. New York: St Martin's Press.

Craik, J. (1994) *The Face of Fashion. Cultural Studies in Fashion*. London: Routledge.

Denzin, N.K. (1992) *Symbolic Interactionism and Cultural Studies*. Cambridge: Blackwell.

Douglas, M. (1970) *Purity and Danger. An Analysis of Concepts of Pollution and Taboo*. Harmondsworth: Penguin.

Duerr, H.P. ([1987] 1994) *Nakenhet och skam: Myten om civilisationsprocessen*. Stockholm/Stehag: Symposion.

Dutton, K.R. (1995) *The Perfectible Body. The Western Ideal of Physical Development*. London: Cassell.

Ebaugh, H.R.F. (1988) *Becoming an EX: The Process of Role Exit*. Chicago: Chicago University Press.

Elias, N. ([1939] 1982) *The Civilizing Process: State Formation and Civilization*. Oxford: Basil Blackwell.

Elias, N. ([1939] 1989) *Sedernas historia. Del I av civilisationsteorin*. Stockholm: Atlantis.

Elias, N. (1991) *The Society of Individuals*. London: Basil Blackwell.

Elias, N. and Dunning, E. (1986) *Från ridderspel till fotbollscup. Sport i sociologisk belysning*. Stockholm: Atlantis.

Eskola, A. ([1971] 1981) *Socialpsykologi*. Stockholm: Almqvist & Wiksell.

Ewen, S. (1988) *All Consuming Images. The Politics of Style in Contemporary Culture*. New York: Basic Books.

Falk, P. (1994) *The Consuming Body*. London: Sage.

Featherstone, M. (1991a) The body in consumer culture, in M. Featherstone, M. Hepworth and B.S. Turner (eds) *The Body: Social Process and Cultural Theory*. London: Sage.

Featherstone, M. (1991b) *Consumer Culture and Postmodernism*. London: Sage.

Featherstone, M. (1994) *Kropp, kultur, konsumtion*. Stockholm/Stehag: Symposion.

Featherstone, M., Hepworth, M. and Turner, B.S. (eds) (1991) *The Body: Social Process and Cultural Theory*. London: Sage.

Fiske, J. (1989) *Understanding Popular Culture*. London: Routledge.

Fonda, J. (1981) *Jane Fondas träningsbok*. Stockholm: PRISMA.

Fonda, J. and McCarthy, M. (1984) *De bästa åren med Jane Fondas mjukträning*. Stockholm: PRISMA.

Fornäs, J. (1991) Narcissus och det Andra. Könsordningens särskiljanden och sammanfogningar, in J. Fornäs, U. Boethius and S. Cwejman (eds) *Kön och Identitet i förändring. Fus-Rapport nr 3*. Stockholm/Stehag: Symposion.

Foucault, M. (1978) *The History of Sexuality, Volume 1*. New York: Pantheon.

Foucault, M. (1979) *Discipline and Punish*. New York: Vintage.

Foucault, M. (1985) *The Use of Pleasure*. New York: Vintage.

Foucault, M. (1986) *The Care of Self*. New York: Pantheon.

Frank, A. (1991) An analytic review, in M. Featherstone, M. Hepworth and B.S. Turner (eds) *The Body: Social Process and Cultural Theory*. London: Sage.

Freud, S. ([1900] 1985) *The Interpretation of Dreams*. Harmondsworth: Penguin.

Freud, S. ([1912] 1986) *Totem and Taboo: Kulturtheoretische Schriften*. Frankfurt am Main: S. Fischer.

Freud, S. ([1914] 1984) On Narcissism, in *On Metapsychology: The Theory of Psychoanalysis*. Harmondsworth: Penguin.

Freud, S. ([1917] 1984) *Mourning and Melancholia. The Pelican Freud Library, Volume 11*. Harmondsworth: Penguin.

Freud, S. ([1920] 1995) *Bortom lustprincipen*. Stockholm: Natur och Kultur.

Freud, S. ([1923] 1984) *The Ego and the Id. The Pelican Freud Library, Volume 11*. Harmondsworth: Penguin.

Freud, S. ([1930] 1986) *Das Unbehagen in der Kultur. Kulturtheoretische Schriften*. Frankfurt am Main: S. Fischer.

Frimodt, J. (1985) *Narcississm: Freud, Kohut, Ziehe*. Göteborg: Vinga Press.

Frisby, D. (1981) *Sociological Impressionism*. London: Routledge.

Frisby, D. (1992) *Simmel and Since. Essays on Georg Simmel's Social Theory*. London: Routledge.

Frisby, D. and Featherstone, M. (1997) *Simmel on Culture*. London: Sage.

Fromm, E. (1969) *Escape from Freedom*. London: Routledge.

Fussel, S. (1991) *Muscle: Confessions of an Unlikely Bodybuilder*. London: Scribner's.

Gaines, C. and Butler, G. (1977) *Pumping Iron: The Art and Sport of Bodybuilding*. London: Sphere.

Giddens, A. (1984) *The Constitution of Society: Outline of the Theory of Structuration*. Cambridge: Polity.

Giddens, A. (1991) *Modernity and Self-Identity. Self and Society in the late Modern Age*. Cambridge: Polity.

Giddens, A. (1992) *The Transformation of Intimacy*. Cambridge: Polity.

Giddens, A. (1994) Living in a post-traditional society, in U. Beck, A. Giddens and S. Lash (eds) *Reflexive Modernization. Politics, Tradition and Aesthetics in the Modern Social Order*. Cambridge: Polity.

Goffman, E. ([1956] 1994) *Jaget och maskerna. En studie i vardagslivets dramatik*. Stockholm: Rabén Prisma.

Goffman, E. (1961) *Asylums. Essays on the Social Situation of Mental Patients and Other Inmates*. Harmondsworth: Penguin.

Goffman, E. ([1961] 1991) *Encounters: Two Essays on the Sociology of Interaction*. New York: Bobs-Merill.

Goffman, E. ([1963] 1972) *Behavior in Public Places. Notes on the Social Organization of Gatherings*. New York: The Free Press.

Goffman, E. ([1967] 1972) *Interaction Ritual: Essays on Face-to-face Behaviour*. London: Penguin.

Goffman, E. (1967) *När människor möts. Studiet av det direkta samspelet mellan människor*. Stockholm: Bonniers.

Green, H. (1986) *Fit for America. Health, Fitness, Sport and American Society*. Baltimore, MD: Johns Hopkins University Press.

Green, T. (1988) *Arnold! The Life of Arnold Schwarzenegger*. London: Star Books.

Grindstaff, L. (1997) Producing trash, class and the money-shot: a behind-the-scenes account of daytime TV talk shows, in J. Lull and S. Hinerman (eds) *Media Scandals*. Cambridge: Polity.

Hall, S. ([1973] 1980) Encoding, decoding, in S. Hall, D. Hobson, A. Love and P. Willis *Culture, Media, Language*. London: Hutchinson.

Hannerz, U. (1969) *Soulside. Inquiries into the Ghetto Culture and Community*. Stockholm: Almqvist & Wiksell.

Haraway, D. (1990) A manifesto for cyborgs: science, technology and socialist feminism in the 1980s, in L.J. Nicholson (ed.) *Feminism/Postmodernism*. New York: Routledge.

Harman, L.D. (1988) *The Modern Stranger. On Language and Membership*. Amsterdam: Mouton de Gruyter.

Hartley, J. (1992) *The Politics of Picture. The Creation of Public in the Age of Popular Media*. London: Routledge.

Haug, F. (ed.) (1992) *Female Sexualization. A Collective Work of Memory*. London: Verso.

Hebdige, D. (1979) *Subculture: The Meaning of Style*. New York: Methuen.

hooks, b. (1992) *Black Looks. Race and Representation*. Boston, MA: Southend Press.

Hornby, N. (1995) *High Fidelity*. Stockholm: Månpocket.

Jeffords, S. (1994) *Hard Bodies. Hollywood Masculinity in the Reagan Era*. New Brunswick, NJ: Rutgers University Press.

Johansson, T. (1994) Narcissism, fragmentering och ontologisk trygghet, *FUS-rapport nr 6, Ungdomskultur i Sverige*. Stockholm/Stehag: Symposion.

Johansson, T. (1995a) Narcissism, kropp och modernitet, *Sociologisk Forskning*, 2: 3–23.

Johansson, T. (1995b) Främlingskap och det främmande. Bodybuilding, kön och identitet, *Kulturella perspektiv*, 4: 19–33.

Johansson, T. (1995c) Narcissism, modernitet och det gåtfulla ansiktet: kulturteoretiska reflektioner, *Nordisk psykologi*, 4: 275–96.

Johansson, T. (1996a) Kultur och kropp: en introduktion, *Sociologisk Forskning*, 2–3: 3–24.

Johansson, T. (1996b) Gendered spaces: the gym culture and the construction of gender, *Young*, 3: 32–47.

Johansson, T. (1996c) *Socialpsykologi och modernitet*. Lund: Studentlitteratur.

Johansson, T. (1998) *Den skulpterade kroppen. Gymkultur, estetik och friskvård*. Stockholm: Carlssons.

Johansson, T. and Miegel, F. (1995) *Kultursociologi*. Lund: Studentlitteratur.

Kellner, D. (1992) *The Persian Gulf TV War*. Boulder: Westview Press.

Kemp, P. (1992) *Emmanuel Lévinas: En introduktion*. Göteborg: Daidalos.

Kernberg, O. ([1975] 1983) *Borderlinetillstånd och patologisk narcissism*. Stockholm: Natur och Kultur.

Klein, A.M. (1990) Little big man: hustling, gender narcissism and the bodybuilding culture, in M.A. Messner and D.F. Sabo (eds) *Sport, Men and the Gender Order. Critical Feminist Perspectives*. Champaign, IL: Human Kinetic Books.

Klein, A.M. (1993a) Of muscle and men, *The Sciences*, November/December.

Klein, A.M. (1993b) *Little Big Men. Bodybuilding Subculture and Gender Construction*. New York: State University of New York Press.

Kohut, H. ([1977] 1986) *Att bygga upp självet*. Stockholm: Natur och Kultur.

Kristeva, J. (1982) *Powers of Horror. An Essay on Abjection*. New York: Columbia University Press.

Kristeva, J. (1991) *Strangers to Ourselves*. New York: Wheatsheaf.

Kuncewiczowa, M. (1976) *En främling*. Lund: Bokád bokförlag AB.

Lacan, J. ([1949] 1989) *Écrits. Spegelstadiet och andra skrifter, i urval av Irene Matthis*. Stockholm: Natur och Kultur.

Laplance, J. and Pontalis, J-B. ([1967] 1988) *The Language of Psychoanalysis*. London: Karnac Books.

Lasch, C. (1984) *Det minimala jaget. Hur man överlever psykiskt i en orolig tid*. Stockholm: Norstedts.

Lasch, C. (1985) *Den narcissistiska kulturen*. Stockholm: Norstedts.

Lévinas, E. ([1948] 1992) *Tiden och den Andre*. Stehag: Symposion.

Lévinas, E. ([1967] 1993) *Etik och oändlighet. Samtal med Philippe Nemo*. Stehag: Symposion.

Levine, D.N. (1985) *The Flight from Ambiguity. Essays in Social and Cultural Theory*. Chicago: The University of Chicago Press.

Lindner, T. (1996) *The Reportage of Urban Culture. Robert Park and the Chicago School*. New York: Cambridge University Press.

Lloyd, M. (1996) Feminism, aerobics and the politics of the body, *Body & Society*, 2: 79–98.

Lull, J. (1991) *China Turned On. Television, Reform and Resistance*. London: Routledge.

Maffesoli, M. (1996) *The Time of the Tribes. The Decline of Individualism in Mass Society*. London: Sage.

Mansfield, A. and McGuinn, B. (1993) Pumping irony: the muscular and the feminine, in S. Scott and D. Morgan (eds) *Body Matters: Essays on the Sociology of the Body*. London: Falmer Press.

Marcuse, H. (1955) *Eros and Civilization: A Philosophical Inquiry Into Freud*. New York: Vintage Books.

Mauss, M. ([1959] 1979) *Sociology and Psychology: Essays*. London: Routledge & Kegan Paul.

McDougal, W. (1908) *Introduction to Social Psychology*. London: Methuen.

McLemore, S.D. (1991) Simmel's 'stranger': a critique of the concept, in L. Ray (ed.) *Formal Sociology of Georg Simmel*. New York: Elgar Reference Collection.

Mead, G.H. ([1932] 1959) *The Philosophy of the Present*. Chicago, IL: Open Court.

Mead, G.H. (1938) *The Philosophy of the Act*. Chicago, IL: University of Chicago Press.

Meltzer, B.N., Petras, J. and Reynolds, L.T. (1975) *Symbolic Interactionism*. London: Routledge.

Meyrowitz, J. (1985) *No Sense of Place*. Harvard, MA: Oxford University Press.

Mosse, G. (1996) *The Image of Men: the Creation of Modern Masculinity*. New York: Oxford University Press.

Neale, S. (1993) Masculinity as spectacle: reflections on men and mainstream cinema, in S. Cohan and I.R. Hark (eds) *Screening the Male: Exploring Masculinities in Hollywood Cinema*. London: Routledge.

Nedelmann, B. (1991) Individualization, exaggeration and paralysation: Simmel's three problems of culture, *Theory, Culture & Society*, 3: 169–93.

Palmblad, E. and Eriksson, B-E. (1995) *Kropp och politik. Hälsoupplysning som samhällssspegel*. Stockholm: Carlssons.

Papastergiadis, N. (1993) *Modernity as Exile. The Stranger in John Berger's Writing*. Manchester: Manchester University Press.

Phillips, A. (1991) *Winnicott*. Stockholm: Wahlström & Widstrand.

Ramström, J. (1991) *Tonåringen i vällfärdssamhället. Om svårigheter att bli vuxen i dagens västerländska kultur*. Stockholm: Natur och Kultur.

Rank, O. ([1914] 1971) *The Double. A Psychoanalytic Study*. Chapel Hill: University of North Carolina Press.

Rank, O. (1941) *Beyond Psychology*. New York: Dover Publications.

Rorty, R. (1989) *Irony, Contingency and Solidarity*. Cambridge: Cambridge University Press.

Ross, E.A. (1908) *Social Psychology*. New York: Macmillan.

Said, E.W. (1978) *Orientalism: Western Conceptions of the Orient*. New York: Pantheon Books.

Schwarzenegger, A. and Hall, D.K. (1974) *Bodyshaping: Styrketräning för kvinnor*. Stockholm: Wahlström & Widstrand.

Sennett, R. ([1977] 1993) *The Fall of Public Man*. Boston: Faber & Faber.

Sernhede, O. (1997) *Ungdomskulturen och de Andra*. Göteborg: Daidalos.

Shilling, C. (1993) *The Body and Social Theory*. London: Routledge.

Sigrell, B. (1994) *Narcissism: ett psykodynamiskt perspektiv*. Stockholm: Natur och Kultur.

Simmel, G. ([1900] 1990) *The Philosophy of Money*. London: Routledge.

Simmel, G. (1908) *Sociology*. Leipzig: Duncker and Humblot.

Simmel, G. ([1908] 1981) Främlingen, in G. Simmel *Hur är samhället möjligt? Och andra essäer*. Göteborg: Korpen.

Simmel, G. ([1911] 1981) Kulturbegreppet och kulturens tragedi, in G. Simmel *Hur är samhället möjligt? Och andra essäer*. Göteborg: Korpen.

Simmel, G. (1950) *The Sociology of Georg Simmel*. New York: The Free Press.

Simmel, G. (1959) *Georg Simmel 1858–1918. A Collection of Essays*. Columbia, OH: Ohio State University Press.

Simmel, G. (1971) *On Individuality and Social Forms*. Chicago, IL: University of Chicago Press.

Stonequist, E.V. (1937) *The Marginal Man. A Study in Personality and Culture Conflict*. New York: Charles Scribner's Sons.

Taylor, T.D. (1997) *Global Pop, World Music, World Markets*. London: Routledge.

Tedeschi, J., Lindskold, S. and Rosenfelt, P. (1985) *Introduction to Social Psychology*. St Paul, MN: West Publishing Company.

Theweleit, K. (1995) *Mansfantasier [Male Fantasies]*. Stockholm: Östlings bokförlag.

Thompson, J.B. (1995) *The Media and Modernity*. Cambridge: Polity.

Thornton, S. (1995) *Club Cultures. Music, Media and Subcultural Capital*. Cambridge: Polity.

Trasher, F. (1927) *The Gang*. Chicago: University of Chicago Press.

Trondman, M. (1994) *Bilden av en klassresa*. Stockholm: Carlssons.

Turner, B.S. (1984) *The Body and Society. Explorations in Social Theory*. London: Blackwell.

Turner, B.S. (1987) *Medical Power and Social Knowledge*. London: Sage.

Turner, B.S. (1992) *Regulating Bodies. Essays in Medical Sociology*. London: Routledge.

Wernick, A. (1991) *Promotional Culture. Advertising, Ideology and Symbolic Expression*. London: Sage.

Whyte, W.F. (1981) *Street Corner Society*. Chicago: University of Chicago Press.

Wilde, O. ([1891] 1972) *The Complete Works of Oscar Wilde*. London: Collins.

Willis, P. (1977) *Learning to Labour*. Aldershot: Gower.

Winnicott, D.W. (1971) *Playing and Reality*. London: Tavistock.

Wirth, L. (1928) *The Ghetto*. Chicago: University of Chicago Press.

Ziehe, T. (1989) Kulturell friställning och narcissistisk sårbarhet, in J. Fornäs, U. Lundberg and O. Sernhede (eds.) *Ungdomskultur – identitet och motstånd*. Stockholm/Stehag: Symposion.

Zorbaugh, H. ([1929] 1978) *The Gold Coast and the Slum. A Sociological Study of Chicago's Near North Side*. Chicago: University of Chicago Press.

Index

SOCIAL CONSTRUCTIONIST PSYCHOLOGY
A CRITICAL ANALYSIS OF THEORY AND PRACTICE

David J. Nightingale and John Cromby (eds)

- How can ideas about the social construction of reality be reconciled with the material and embodied aspects of our being?
- How can a realist framework inform social constructionist research?
- What are the limits of social constructionism?

This book explores the growing conviction that dominant 'discursive' trends in social constructionism – which deal with the analysis of language and discourse to the exclusion of the material world, embodiment, personal-social history, and power – are inadequate or incomplete and risk preventing social constructionism from maturing into a viable and coherent body of theory, method and practice. In highlighting what are seen as deficiencies in current constructionist approaches, the book inevitably takes a somewhat critical stance. However, the contributing authors are committed to a constructionist analysis of the human condition – into which they seek to reintegrate the material and embodied aspects of our nature. This accessible text draws together for the first time a wider range of emerging issues, ideas and discussions in constructionist psychology. It shows how these issues are relevant to everyday life, using carefully chosen examples to illustrate its arguments, and provides a coherent and challenging introduction to the field.

Contents
What's wrong with social constructionism? – Part I: A critical analysis of theory – Critical reflexive humanism and critical constructionist psychology – Beyond appearances: a critical realist approach to social constructionist work – A paradigm shift? Connections with other critiques of social constructionism – Part II: Materiality and embodiment – Between the dark and the light: power and the material contexts of social relations – 'Discourse or materiality?' Impure alternatives for recurrent debates – Discourse and the embodied person – The extra-discursive in social constructionism – Realism, constructionism and phenomenology – Taking our selves seriously – Part III: A critical analysis of practice – Whose construction? Points from a feminist perspective – Social constructionism: implications for psychotherapeutic practice – That's all very well, but what use is it? – Conclusion – Reconstructing social constructionism – Glossary – Index.

256 pp   0 335 20192 X (paperback)   0 335 20193 8 (hardback)

POSTMODERNITY
Second Edition

David Lyon

> . . . written with enthusiasm and a commitment to clarity . . . Lyon shows that the employment of a sociological imagination can add new and unexpected depth to cultural analyses.
>
> Keith Tester, University of Portsmouth

- What does 'postmodernity' mean? How does it help us grasp the meaning of 'modernity'? Is it better than similar terms such as 'high', or 'late', or 'reflexive' modernity?
- What are the enduring social consequences of the widespread diffusion of communication and information technologies and of consumer-oriented lifestyles?
- Does being postmodern mean that 'anything goes', or are values and beliefs still socially significant?

In the second edition of this highly successful text, postmodernity is seen as the social condition of the twenty-first century, in which some of the most familiar features of the modern world are not only called into question, but actually undermined by novel trends. The key carriers of the postmodern – new technologies and consumerism – emerged in thoroughly modern contexts, but so profoundly affect everyday social life that modernity itself is changing shape.

Postmodernity is explored as a theoretical concept in order to uncover and illuminate central social trends of the present. Its historical roots and cultural dimensions are examined, as are the ideas of its leading theorists. In this updated and expanded edition, greater attention is paid to processes of globalization as well as to the postmodern view of cyberspace, cyborgs, and the body as a site of moral conflict.

Contents
Preface to the first edition – Preface to the second edition – Introduction: screen replicants and social realities – Postmodernity: the history of an idea – Modernity and its discontents – From postindustrialism to postmodernity – Consumerism and beyond: the shape(lessness) of things to come – Postmodernity, Fin de Millénaire *and the future – Notes – Index.*

144 pp   0 335 20144 X (paperback)   0 335 20145 8 (hardback)

MODERNITY AND POSTMODERN CULTURE

Jim McGuigan

- What is postmodern culture?
- Do modern values still matter?
- Why is everyday life now apparently more liberated than in the past yet, at the same time, strangely disconcerting?

Modernity and Postmodern Culture is a critical introduction to claims concerning the postmodernization of culture and society. Contemporary culture may be 'postmodern' in the sense of fluidity of meaning, changing power relations and commodification in art, entertainment and everyday life, but modernity persists in the dynamics of capitalist civilization, albeit in an increasingly reflexive mode characterized by widespread uncertainty about social existence, progress and rationality.

The theories of Baudrillard, Beck, Castells, Giddens, Habermas, Haraway, Jameson, Lyotard and others on the contemporary scene are discussed, and specific issues concerning architecture, theme parks, screen culture, science, technology and the environment are examined. Jim McGuigan argues that there have been tensions between instrumental and critical reason throughout the history of modernity that are still being played out. He questions the irrationalist tendencies and the accommodative attitude to prevailing conditions of much postmodern thought, and insists upon the enduring relevance of the Enlightenment tradition to social and cultural analysis.

Contents
Series editor's foreword – Acknowledgements – Introduction – Declaring the postmodern – Modernity: a contradictory project – Scrambled images – Fractured identities – The information age – Reflexive modernity – Conclusion – Glossary – References – Index.

192 pp   0 335 19915 1 (paperback)   0 335 19916 X (hardback)